SEURAT
BATHERS AT ASNIÈRES

ALASTAIR SOOKE

National Gallery Global, London
Distributed by Yale University Press

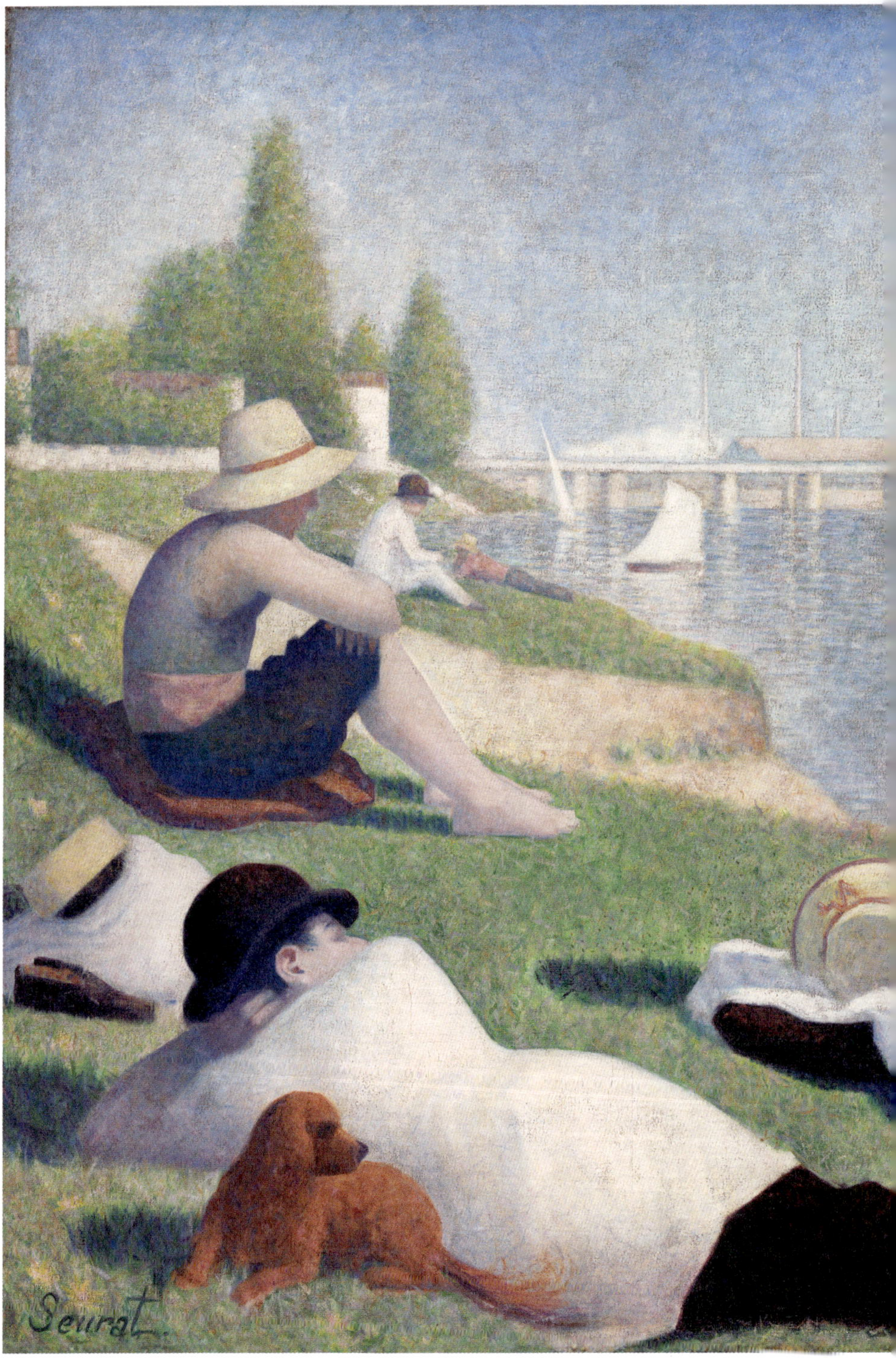
Seurat

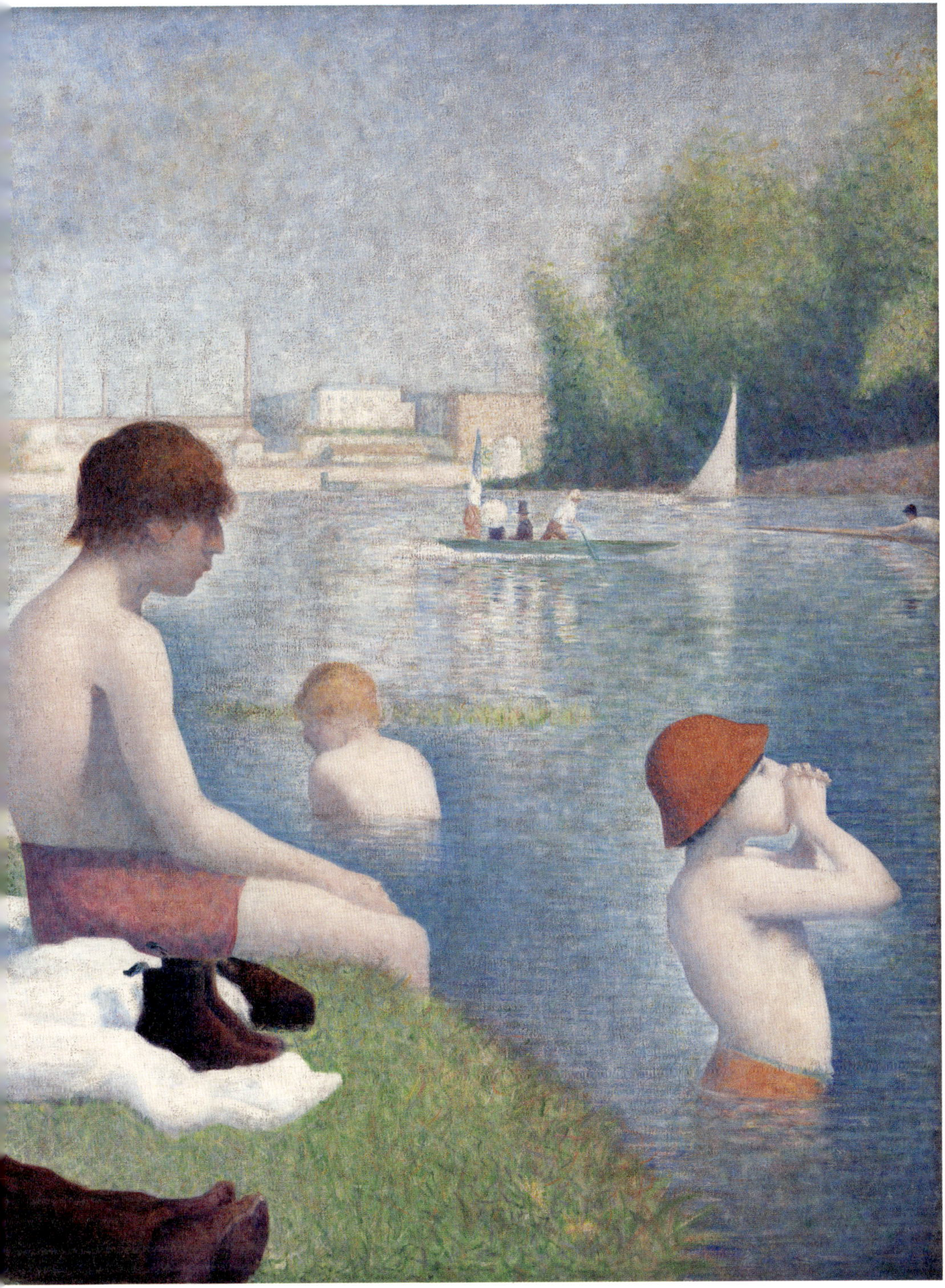

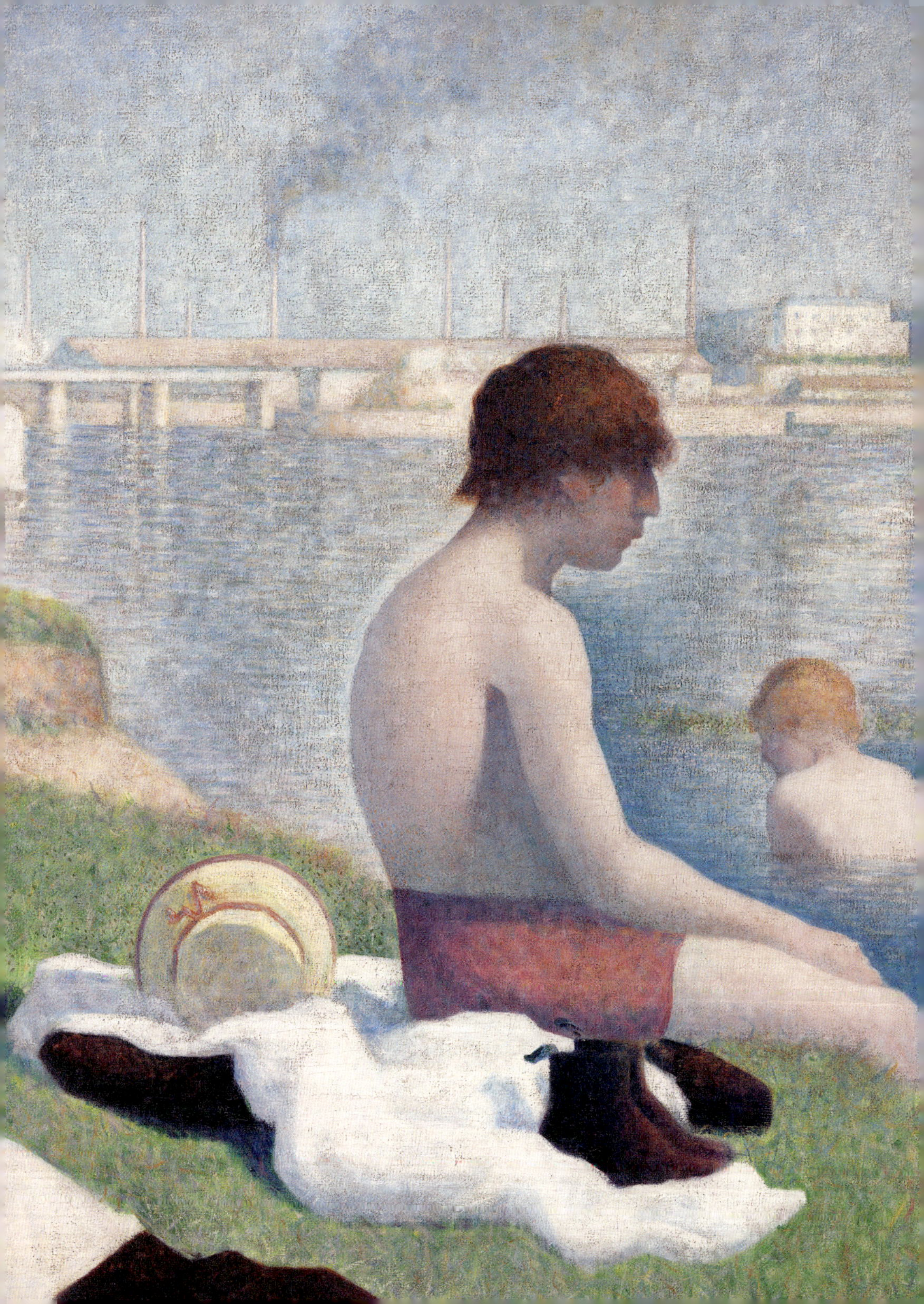

A SUMMERTIME EPIPHANY

On a grassy, sunlit riverbank, several men and boys are whiling away the day (fig. 1). Sailboats bob around in the water, but, in truth, the spot they've picked isn't especially picturesque. A distant locomotive cloaked in its own steam crosses a railway bridge. A dark smudge of smoke rises from the chimney of a pink factory before merging with the atmospheric haze. Still, with almost disconsolate determination, these fellows attempt to relax. A few wear hats – chocolate-coloured bowlers, wide-brimmed boaters – to protect themselves from the sun. A bare-armed lad, sporting a pink sash around his waist, has arranged his baggy maroon trousers above his knees and places two unshod feet flat on the yellowish, scratchy-looking turf. Three more youths have already stripped off. One, facing away from us, is partially submerged (immersed, in fact, up to his nipples); another, dressed in an odd sun helmet like a flower pot, raises both hands to his mouth, as if hollering at someone we can't see on the river or opposite bank. (Or maybe he's just relishing the reverberation of his 'halloo' across the water.) Something – or the person he's shouting at, perhaps – has caught the attention of a frisky little dog with a wispy tail like a bedraggled brush.

1 *Bathers at Asnières*, 1884
Oil on canvas, 201 × 300 cm
The National Gallery, London

The dog sits on the shore beside a fully dressed man who is lying down.

But it's the third bather – a hunched figure with frizzy gingery hair and an aquiline nose, perched on the bank's edge (and presumably dangling his toes in the river) – who, positioned centrally, dominates this view. The clothes he has shed appear behind him like a pool of melting gelato: an expanse of sparkling linen above what must be chestnut trousers; and, like the remnants of two chocolate flakes in soft ice cream, a pair of brown boots that, thanks to their seemingly lapping, tongue-like tabs, emanate almost as much energy as that alert dog swivelling its muzzle. And let's not forget his beribboned straw hat, which, evidently, in the heat, has flattened his sweaty hairdo; like those boot tabs and the russet dog's whisking tail, its fluttery little bow provides a perky ornamental note. Embedded in the voluptuous white ripples of his upper garment, it rests at an improbably perpendicular angle, as if balancing on its rim – like a discus that, still quivering, has just struck the ground. The concentric semicircles its shape creates echo the smaller white circle of a parasol in a distant boat, obscuring a woman in dark attire, who sits beside her top-hatted companion. The two of them sit beside a furled French tricolour, as a third figure rows.

A high summer scene, then; but, while the sun may be beaming, these men at leisure aren't. Try as you might, you won't discern a smile. It's hard to make out any of their mouths at all (fig. 2). That of the reclining figure in the foreground is hidden by his shoulder; the lips of the boy calling out are likewise concealed, in his case by his hands. As for the others, their faces are either semi-obscured by shadow, or too far away. We register something, it's true, of the features in profile of the silhouetted central bather, but his protruding upper lip hardly suggests a grin. And what should we make of his slumped, world-weary posture? If he's a pleasure-seeker, he's yet, it seems, to find any fun. Several others appear similarly sun-dazed and downcast.

2 *Study for 'Bathers at Asnières'*, 1883–4
Oil on wood, 15.2 × 25 cm
The National Gallery, London

3 *Clothes on the Grass: Study for 'Bathers at Asnières'*, 1883
Oil on wood, 16.2 × 24.8 cm
The National Gallery, London
On loan from Tate

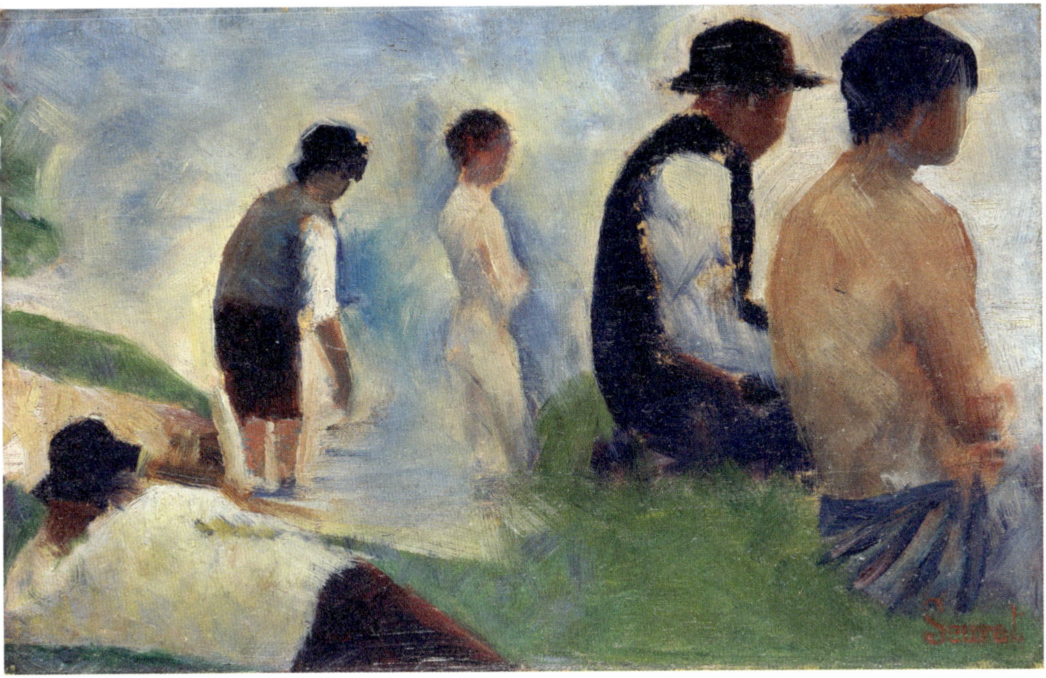
Seurat

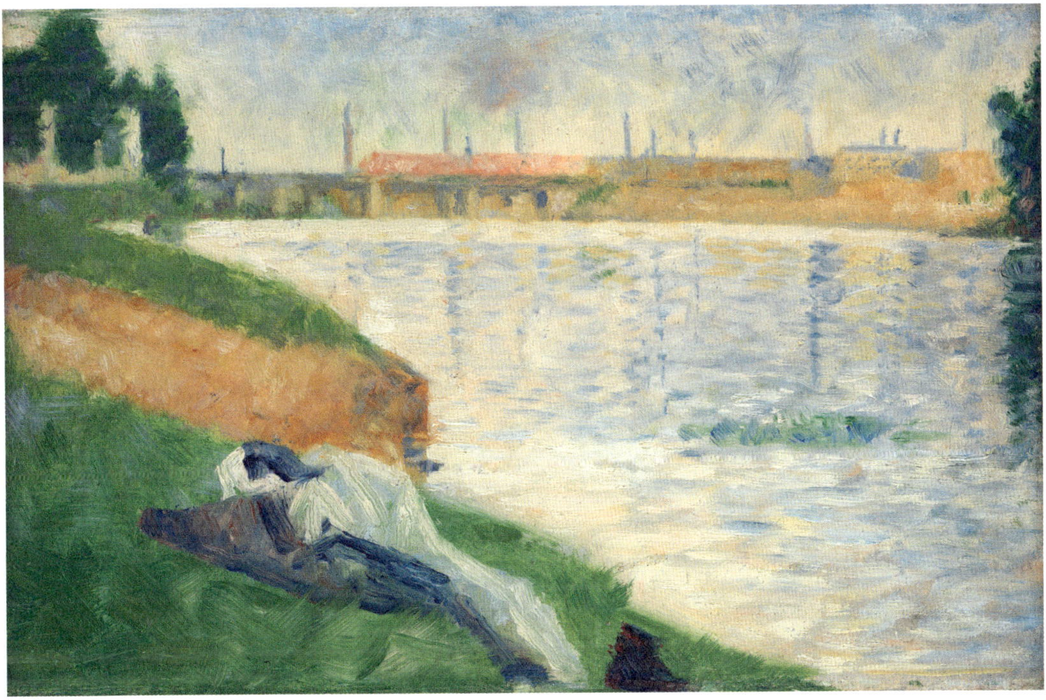

The purplish quality of the strangely smooth and waxy skin on display doesn't exactly lift the mood. These aren't hale and hearty, suntanned specimens of athletic manhood.

The faint air of melancholy is amplified by this gathering's curiously atomised, even alienated, nature. No one regarding these clustered sun-seekers would describe them as convivial. Do they even know each other? Apart from the boy, who's anyway yelling at somebody offstage (if he's shouting at someone at all), nobody interacts; aside from a couple of distant oarsmen – and, of course, that watchful dog – only the youth crying through his fists as if blowing a conch shell is at all animated. Each figure appears isolated, mired in his own thoughts. Like spectators in the cheap seats, half-concentrating on a performance, they seem indifferent to the everyday drama in front of them. Perhaps, as that far-off factory reminds us (fig. 3), they'll soon be back at work. (Is this why everyone's so glum?) Theirs is the listless body language of clock-watching, not larking about. Amid so much stasis, even solemnity, the action of that whooping youngster has the force of a revelation. But what does this epiphany mean?

METHOD-MADE 'POETRY'

On the day that I visit the National Gallery to study the oil painting that represents this scene – *Bathers at Asnières* (1884), by the short-lived French painter and draughtsman Georges Seurat – I find it hanging in an imposing gilded frame, against a grey wall and above green marble skirting, as delighted visitors ebb and flow, taking pictures on smartphones. The first thing that strikes you about it is its size. It's massive: more than 2 metres high, and exactly 3 metres across. And it seems even more colossal compared with another, smaller artwork by Seurat in the collection, *Le Bec du Hoc, Grandcamp* (fig. 4). This depicts a dramatic outcrop – like a great, ominous cresting wave or rock monster's maw – that, until it was bombarded

4 *Le Bec du Hoc, Grandcamp,* 1885
Oil on canvas, 64.8 × 81.6 cm
On loan from Tate: Purchased 1952

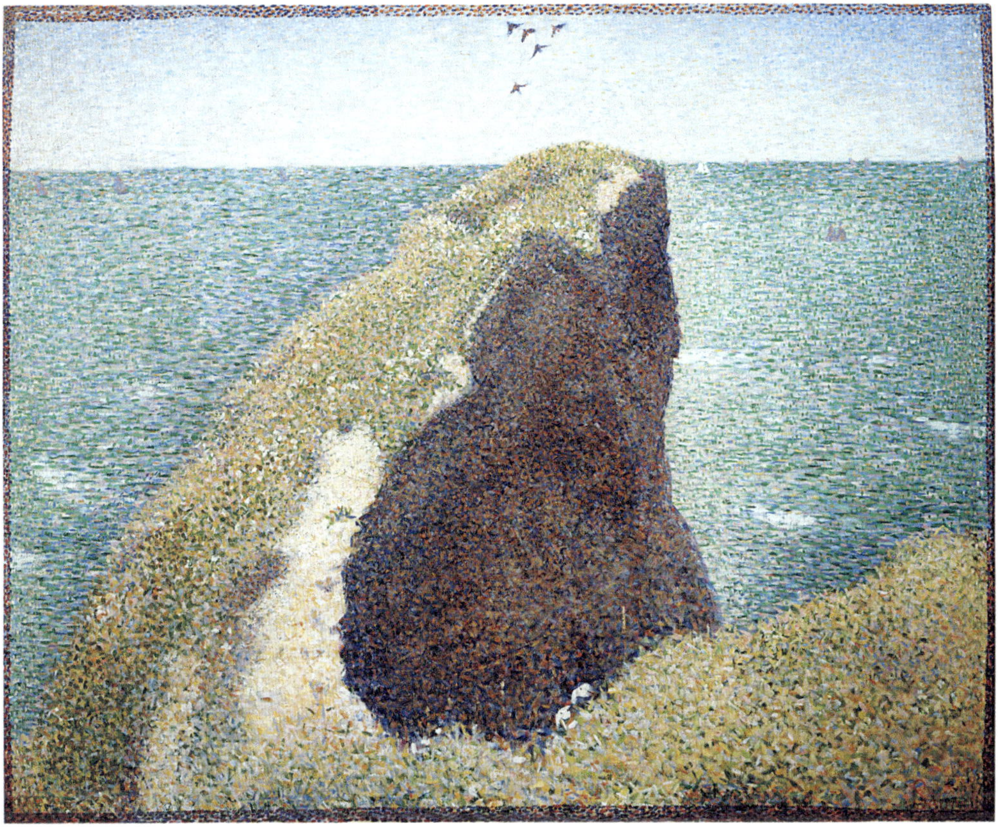

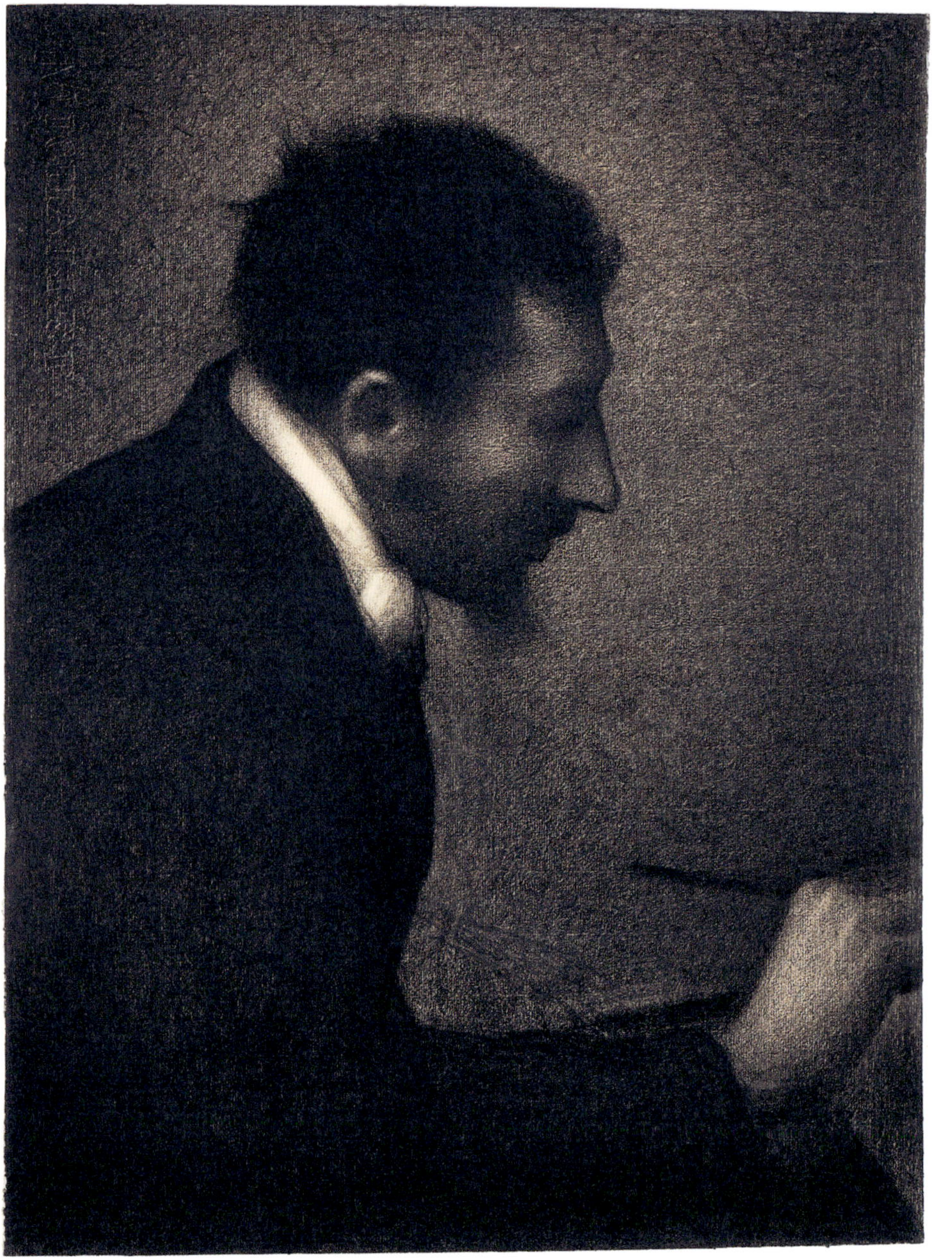

during the Second World War, dominated the Normandy coast where this Parisian artist often painted during the summer. Yet, the central figure in the *Bathers*, whose back traces a similar curve, dwarfs this geologically huge motif. Even to those unfamiliar with Seurat and his oeuvre, it's apparent from its scale that *Bathers at Asnières* is an ambitious work of art, designed to make a public statement. It has the immediate impact – the charisma – of those grand, supersized canvases liberally distributed elsewhere in the gallery. It feels important.

Seurat wanted this painting, which he titled *Une baignade, Asnières*, to be shown at the Paris Salon, the foremost and (largely) annual official showcase of predominantly French art, to which he submitted it for the jury's consideration in the spring of 1884. He'd already exhibited at the Salon (albeit only once), the previous year, when his virtuosic crayon portrait of an artist friend lost in concentration (fig. 5) was picked out by an art critic who called it 'an excellent study in light and dark, a meritorious drawing that cannot be the work of a newcomer'.[1] Yet, for reasons that haven't been recorded, the Salon rejected Seurat's *Bathers*. It still appeared before the public that year, as part of an open exhibition arranged by the newly formed and progressive Groupe des Artistes Indépendants, which took place inside a wooden structure in the Cour des Tuileries by the Louvre. According to the twentieth-century British art historian and collector Douglas Cooper, this was 'the great artistic event in Paris in 1884', in which more than 400 artists, each of whom had the right to exhibit two pictures, took part.[2] But, perhaps because it was so big, Seurat's painting was hung unfavourably in the buffet and attracted little press. Those who did notice it mocked it. The French writer Paul Alexis, a friend of both the novelist Emile Zola and the artist Paul Cezanne, declared that, while Seurat's *Baignade* was 'ridiculous', the 'earnestness' of its execution was 'almost moving, and I can hardly bring myself to make fun of it'.[3] Seemingly, in 1884, the gravitas

5 *Aman-Jean (Portrait of Edmond François Aman-Jean)*, 1882–3
Conté crayon on Michallet paper, 62.2 × 47.5 cm
The Metropolitan Museum of Art, New York. Bequest of Stephen C. Clark, 1960

that Seurat's *Bathers* transmits today within the impressive setting of the National Gallery wasn't yet apparent.[4] The story of its initial rejection, subsequent relegation to a bar and public ridicule seems like an open-and-shut case, in the oft-told history of avant-garde French painting, of the so-called 'shock of the new'.

Yet, as we have seen, *Bathers at Asnières* is an ambitious work – as underlined by the comparative modesty of the drawing shown by Seurat at the Salon of 1883 – and, at this point, it's worth noting that, when it was first exhibited, the artist was only 24 years old. Why does this matter? For two reasons. First, it reveals that Seurat had already attained considerable artistic maturity by his early twenties; there aren't many young painters who could pull off a composition like this, imbued with so much poetry, and on such a scale, with such aplomb. Second, this fact reminds us that we should refrain from considering this painting in the light of artistic decisions taken later in Seurat's career, since *Bathers at Asnières* is the first of six vast canvases that he produced prior to his early death, at the age of 31, during an epidemic of diphtheria.[5] (He also left behind 60 smaller paintings, about 170 wood panels and 275 drawings.)

For, despite the enduring popularity of modern French painting, Seurat suffers something of an image problem. He retains his reputation as the inventor of a seemingly impersonal painting technique known as 'Pointillism', a quasi-scientific method derived from nineteenth-century colour theory. This involved applying tiny, separate patches of pure pigment directly to the canvas; when viewed from a distance, these were meant to fuse together to create new hues in the beholder's eye. (In fact, this doesn't happen, but the cumulative effect of a Pointillist painting's myriad specks is typically luminous and shimmering.) Seurat is still known as the painter of interminable dots – a hallmark of the late nineteenth-century avant-garde movement of Neo-Impressionism, with which he was already associated during his lifetime. To his detractors, even today, these dots can appear as off-putting as a rash. As an artist, he supposedly developed a distinctive, automatic formula ('It's done mechanically?' one visitor to an 1894 Neo-Impressionist exhibition reportedly asked, before his companion informed him, 'No, Monsieur, by hand').[6] And, at least in the popular imagination, he remained in thrall to it to the end.

Almost a century ago, the British art critic Roger Fry cemented this reputation by characterising Seurat as a 'strange young man' with a 'passion for logical abstraction' and 'an almost mathematical precision of mind'. Beneath his 'rigorous intellect and reserved manner', Fry wrote, Seurat maintained a 'fanatical devotion' to his system of slowly accumulating upon the canvas 'minute dots of colour'.[7] This description seems to tally with contemporary accounts of Seurat's taciturn aloofness, as well as a photograph of him in which, neatly dressed in a buttoned-up jacket (from which, behind his beard, a cravat suitably decorated with Pointillist dots erupts), he appears as standoffish and stiff as an ancient Egyptian scribe (fig. 6). Or perhaps a 'notary', the nickname that, according to one friend, the Symbolist poet and art critic Gustave Kahn, was given to him 'in a moment of humour' by the older Impressionist painter Edgar Degas.[8] Seurat appears again, looking more like the fanatic of Fry's description, in a dramatically up-lit, even ectoplasmic likeness in black pencil from 1883, by another friend, the artist Ernest Joseph Laurent (fig. 7). Seurat himself wasn't averse to propagating this myth: 'People see poetry in what I do', he told the Neo-Impressionist French painter Charles Angrand. 'No, I apply my method and that's all.'[9]

Except, in the case of his *Bathers*, that's not all, because this 'method' hadn't yet been devised – if, indeed, any such prescriptive system may be divined in Seurat's art (and many recent writers have downplayed its supposedly scientific tendencies, emphasising instead the artist's spontaneity).[10] If you scrutinise the canvas, you will find dots only in certain areas. A swarm of them, like gnats, seems to buzz about

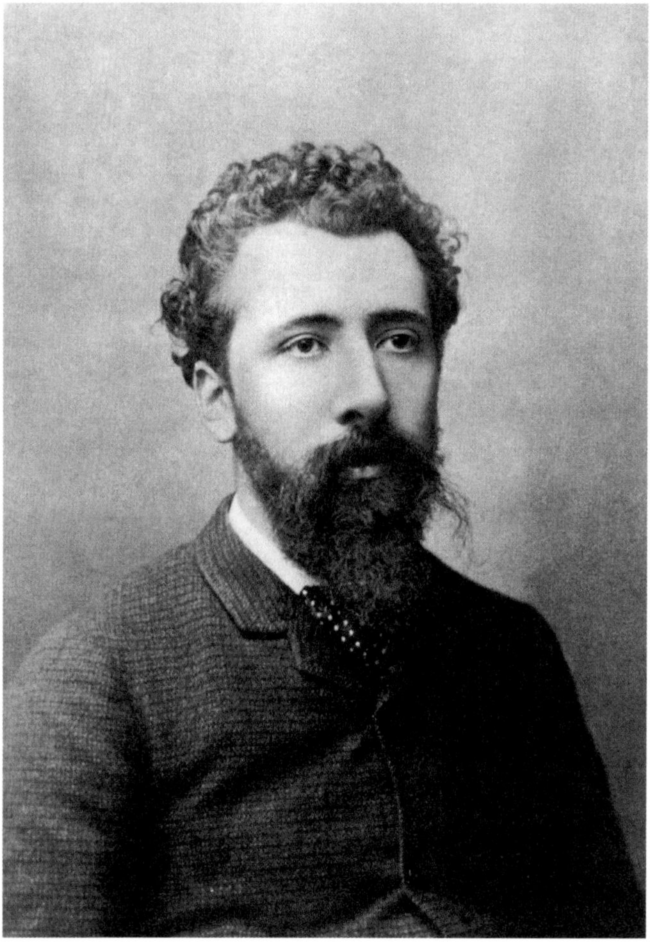

6 Seurat in about 1888, photographer unknown

7 Ernest Joseph Laurent (1859–1929)
Portrait of Georges Seurat, 1883
Black pencil on laid paper, 38.7 × 28.5 cm
Musée du Louvre, Paris

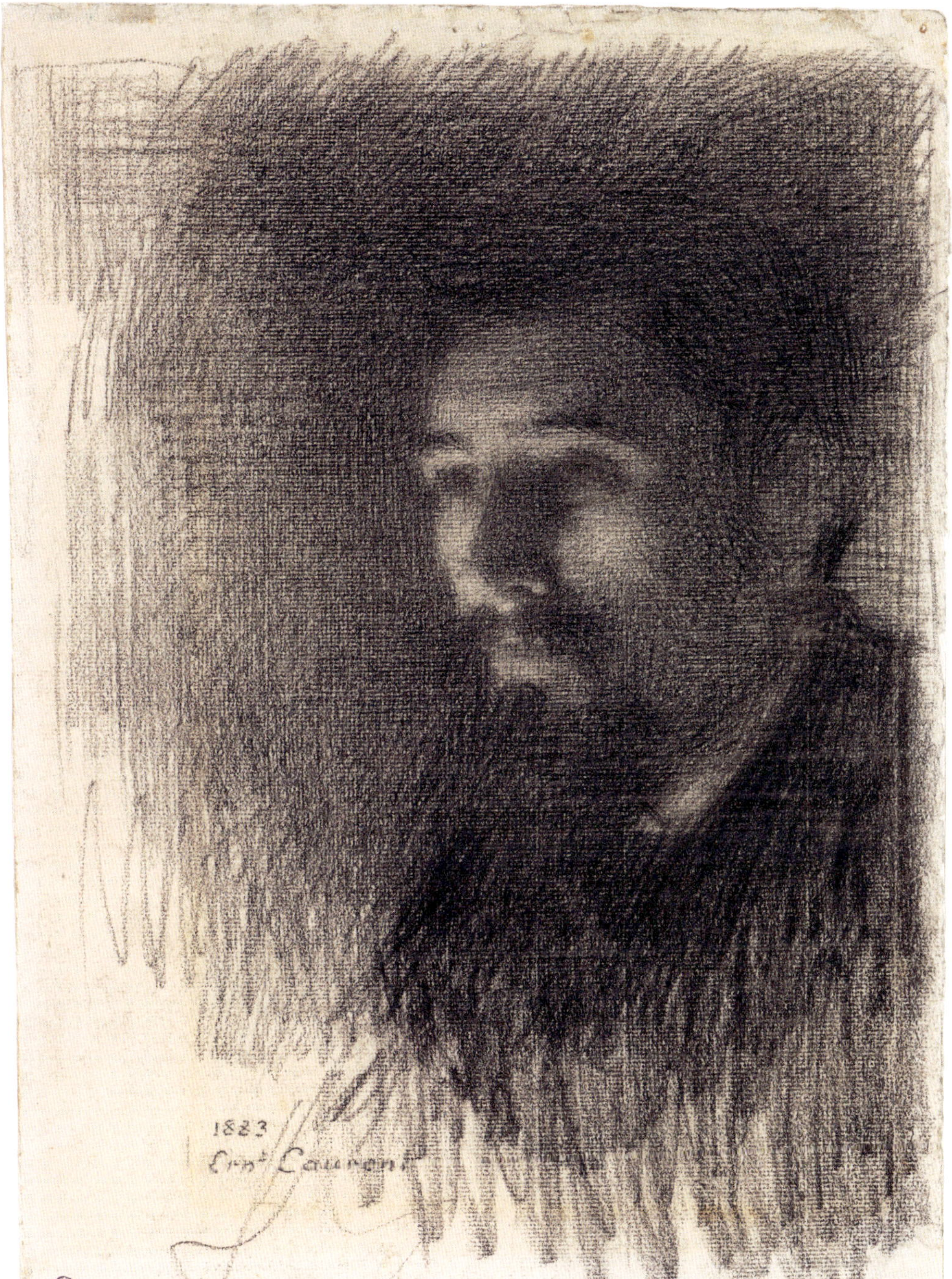
1883
Ernt Laurent

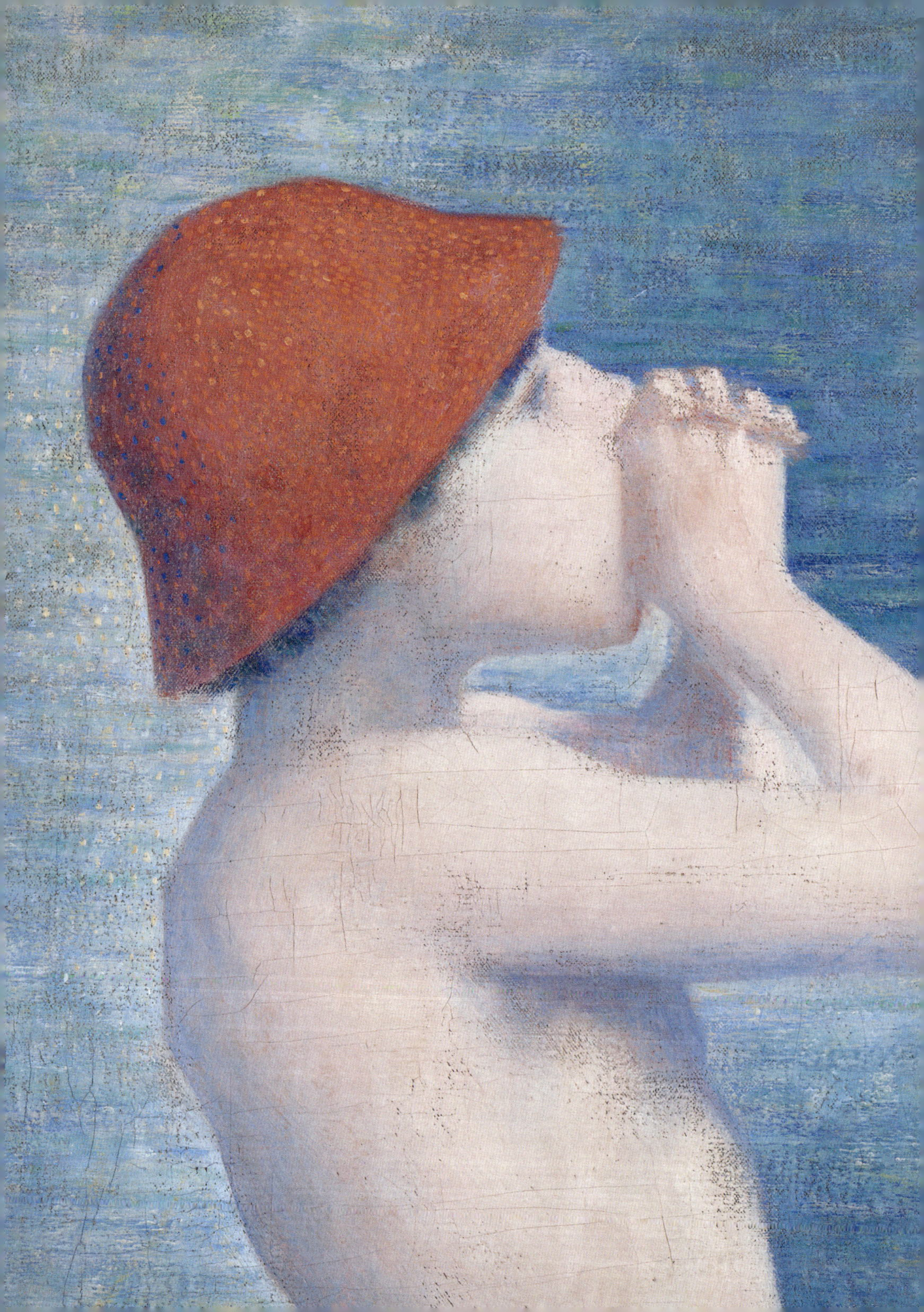

8 Detail of *Bathers at Asnières*: brushstrokes visible on boy's hat

the rim of that central bather's boater. Minuscule round markings in orange and blue speckle the headgear of the hollering boy (fig. 8), as if it were the oversized carapace of some yet-to-be-discovered ladybird or other species of beetle; more spots and flecks, now yellow, like glittering confetti, cascade from this youth's hat and down his back, imbuing him with an ecstatic air. Since Seurat's 'method' only crystallised after he'd completed the *Bathers*, this must be later retouching. If, then, *Bathers at Asnières* isn't a Pointillist painting, how should we think of it? And why, in 1884, at a still-tentative stage in Seurat's career, did a picture of such scope and proportions emerge – and one, to boot, which initially seemed so peculiar that it wrong-footed its earliest viewers? To answer these questions, we must consider his early life and artistic development.

BECOMING AN ARTIST

Georges-Pierre Seurat was born in Paris on 2 December 1859. From the age of three, he grew up in the tenth arrondissement, in a fourth-floor apartment with six rooms on the boulevard de Magenta, created as part of Baron Haussmann's mid-nineteenth-century renovation of the city. The iron railing running along the apartment's balcony sometimes appears in Seurat's early drawings: in *On the Balcony* (1882–3, Musée du Louvre, Paris), for instance, its swirling volutes form a heart-like shape beside the silhouetted profile of a woman (perhaps the artist's mother) sewing or concentrating on a book. Seurat had two older siblings: a brother, Emile, who was already a teenager by the time of Georges's birth and who, supported by his family, later pursued a career as a playwright; and a sister, Marie-Berthe, who, when Georges was six, married an industrial engineer, Léon Appert, whose specialism – stained glass – may have influenced the artist's early fascination with the properties of colour. (Seurat's interest in industrial architecture – In 1889 he painted the Eiffel Tower before it had been finished – has

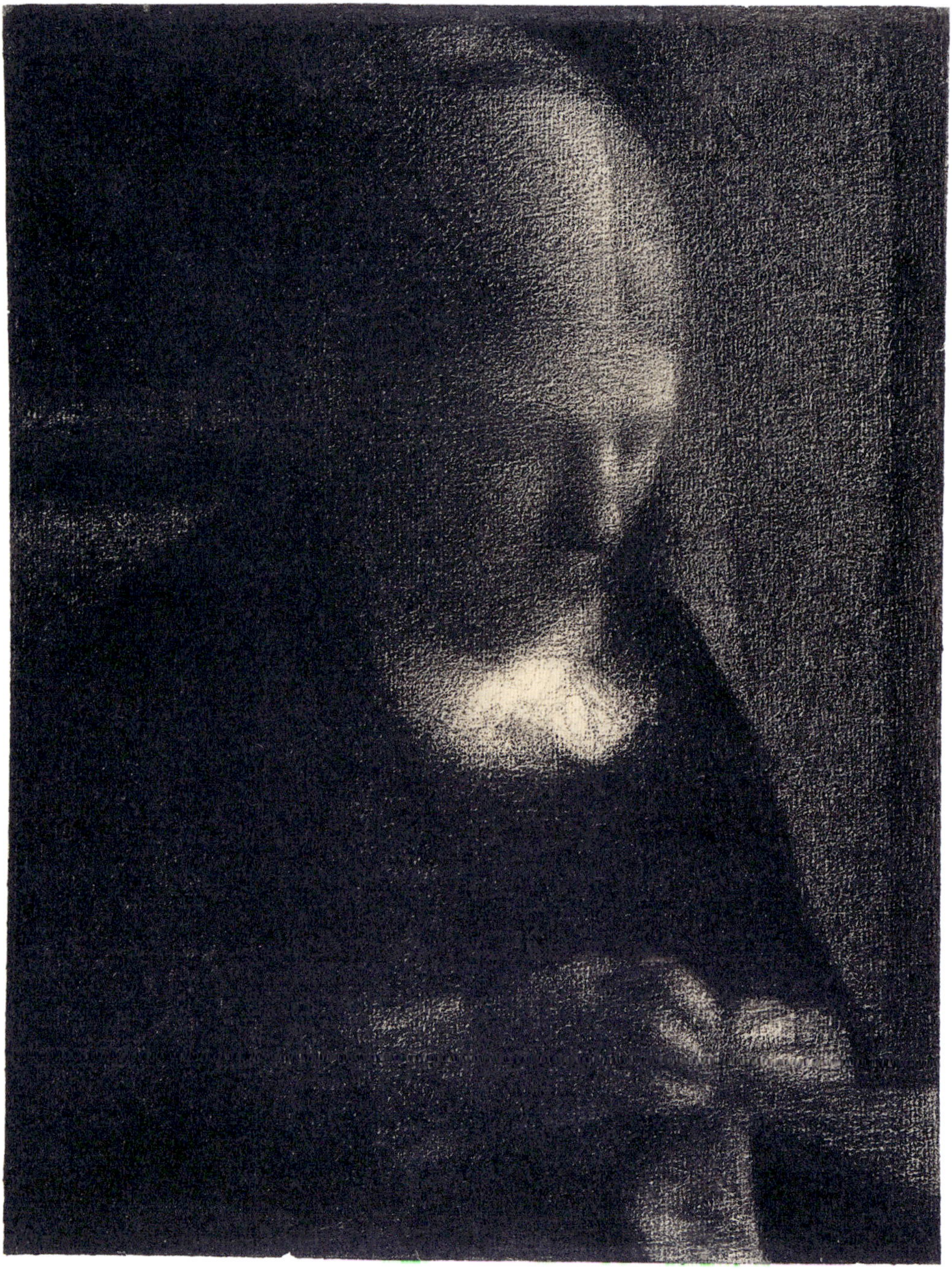

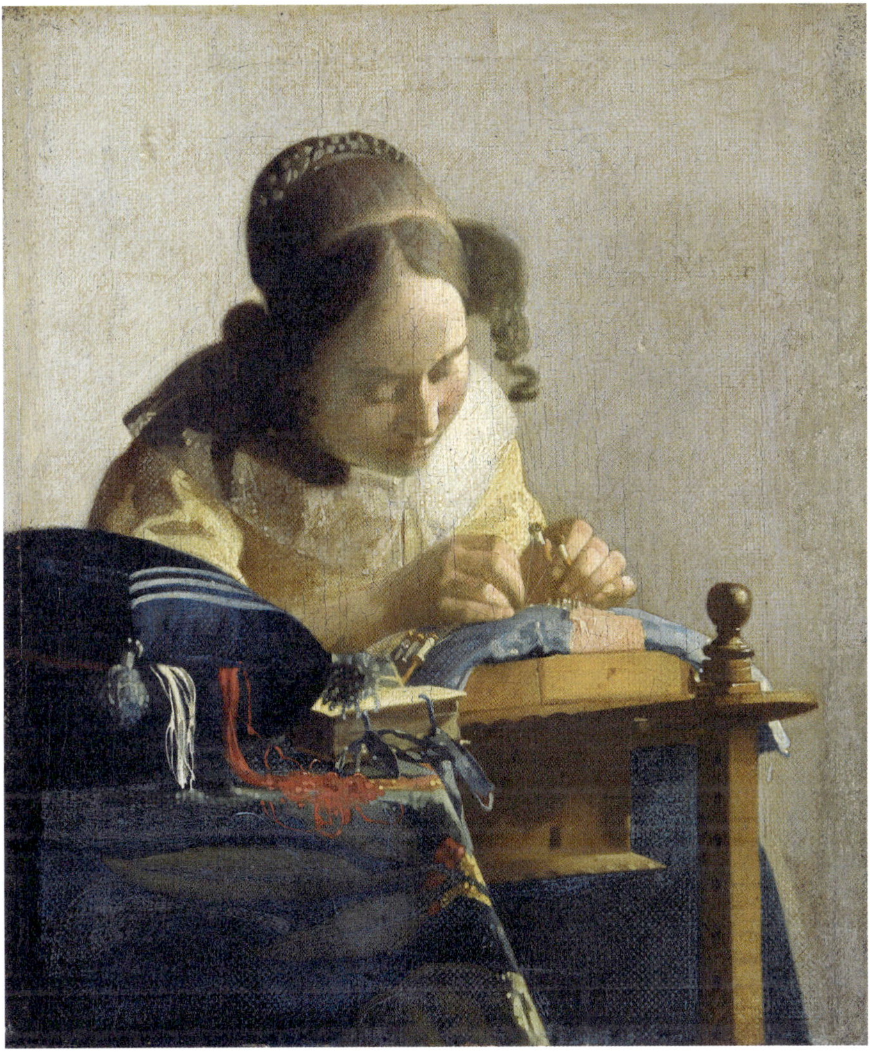

9 *Embroidery; The Artist's Mother*, 1882–3
Conté crayon on Michallet paper,
31.2 × 24.1 cm
The Metropolitan Museum of Art, New York. Purchase, Joseph Pulitzer Bequest, 1951; acquired from The Museum of Modern Art, Lillie P. Bliss Collection

10 Johannes Vermeer (1632–1675)
The Lacemaker, 1669/70
Oil on canvas glued on wood,
24 × 21 cm
Musée du Louvre, Paris

also been linked to Appert's presence in his family.) There was another, younger sibling, François-Gabriel, born in 1863, who died by the age of five. At this point, because his father, Antoine – a court bailiff, who'd retired early after speculating successfully in property – spent much of his time in a suburban villa apart from his wife, Seurat effectively became an only child in a household run by women. His mother, Ernestine Faivre, came from a Parisian family of artisans and likely encouraged Seurat's art. She was very close to her widowed sister, Anaïs Faivre Haumonté, whose husband had owned a department store.

In a couple of drawings made around 1883, Seurat depicts his parents. In one, *Man Dining* (1883–4, private collection), his father appears as an indistinct and remote presence with a white napkin tucked into his collar, seemingly more interested in gobbling his dinner than interacting with his son. In the other, *Embroidery; The Artist's Mother* (fig. 9), Ernestine's pose evokes that of the woman in *The Lacemaker* (fig. 10) by the Dutch artist Johannes Vermeer, which Seurat must have encountered at the Louvre. The mood of this second drawing is more intimate and sympathetic, and reflects both Ernestine's peaceful composure, as the centre of the household, and the love felt for her by her son. Years later, even after he'd become involved with Madeleine Knobloch (fig. 11), his mistress (with whom he had two sons), Seurat still returned most evenings to the apartment on the boulevard de Magenta to share a meal with his mother.

According to family tradition, Seurat – who, as a young man, was said by Kahn to be 'crazy about drawing' – was taken on sketching trips by his uncle, Paul Haumonté, an amateur painter. By 1876, Seurat was attending drawing lessons at a municipal school near his home run by the sculptor Justin Lequien, where he met the artist Aman-Jean, the subject of that portrait accepted by the Salon (see fig. 5). Two years later, in February 1878, Seurat sat the entrance examinations for the Ecole des Beaux-Arts, which predicated

11 *Young Woman powdering Herself*, 1888–90
Oil on canvas, 95.5 × 79.5 cm
The Courtauld Gallery, London

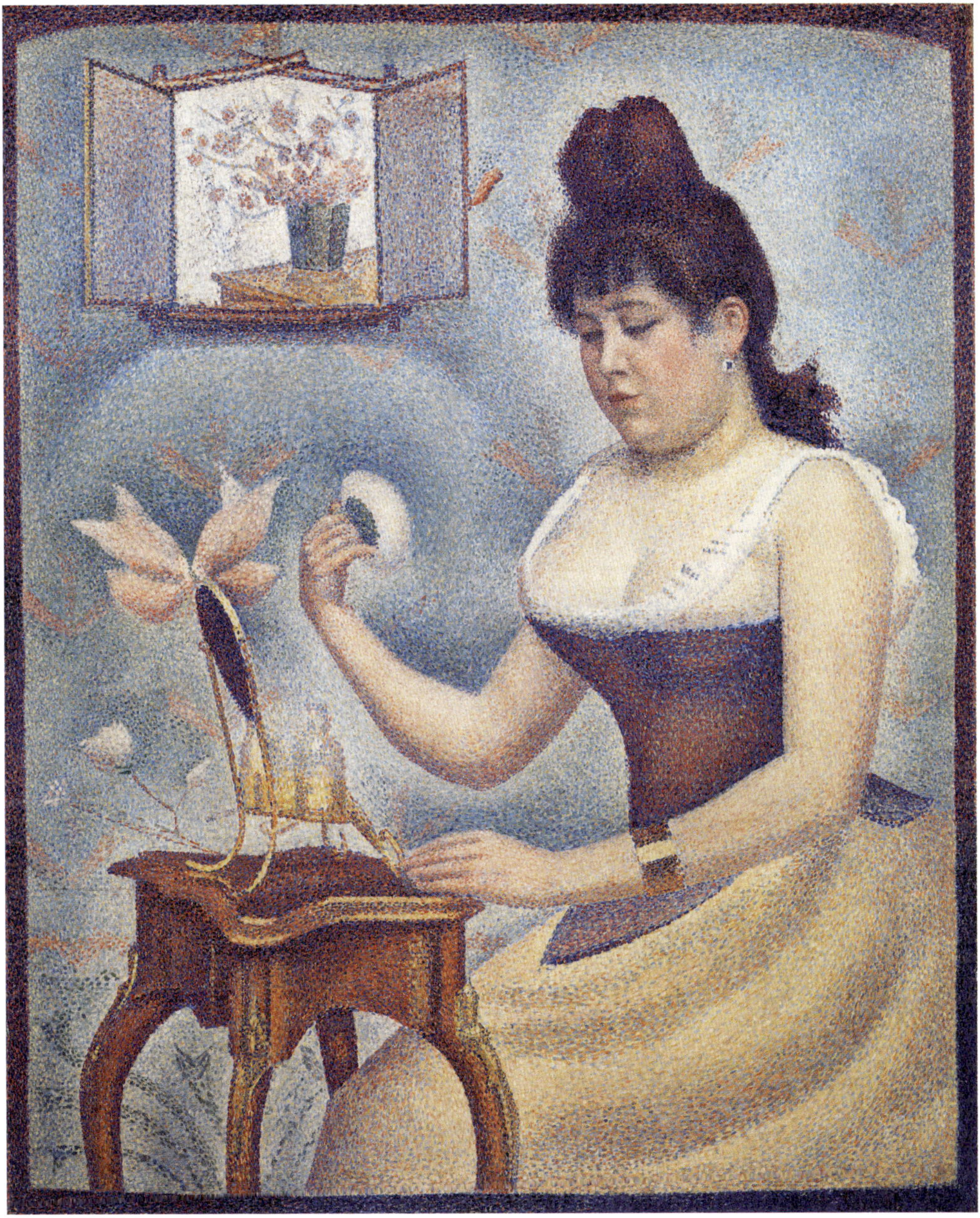

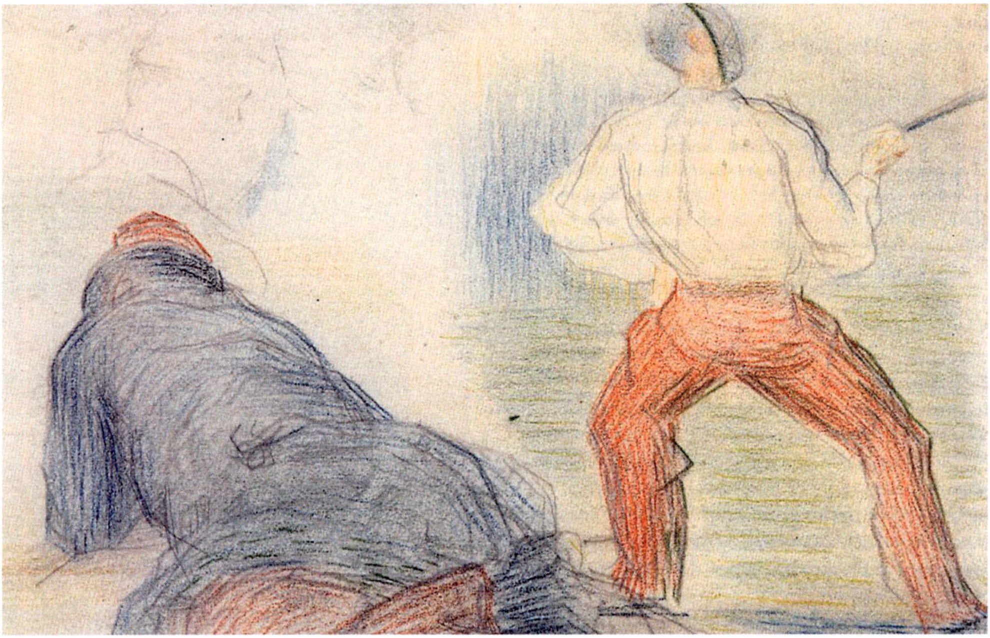

12 *Soldier fencing*, 1880 (from the so-called Brest sketchbook)
Graphite and coloured pencils on white wove paper, 14.7 × 23.2 cm
Private collection

its teaching upon classical precepts, and enrolled in the studio of the strict German-born painter Henri Lehmann. Lehmann was a true-hearted pupil of the great Neoclassical painter Jean-Auguste-Dominique Ingres, whose work Seurat copied as a student. (He also made drawings after Raphael, Hans Holbein the Younger and Nicolas Poussin, whose composition *The Finding of Moses*, now held at the Musée du Louvre, Paris, may have been a source for the *Bathers*.) Under Lehmann's instruction, Seurat received an orthodox academic training, copying plaster casts of antique statues, as well as classic pieces by the old masters, and working from life models. For an artist who would later be considered avant-garde, it was a conservative start. It was also an underwhelming one: in 1879, he was ranked only 47th in Lehmann's 70-strong class. By the end of that year, during which Seurat may have visited the Fourth Impressionist Exhibition with Aman-Jean and Laurent (who'd both followed him to Lehmann's studio), he'd left Paris for the city of Brest in Brittany, to undertake military service.

A sketchbook containing 56 drawings in pencil and coloured crayon dates from his time in Brest. In one sheet (fig. 12), he studies the pose of a fencing soldier wearing reddish trousers; a separate figure reclines – a little like the figure in the foreground of the *Bathers*. In another, Seurat depicts a seated soldier, this time dressed in a blue tunic with prominent pink epaulettes. Yet their slightly droopy quality, coupled with the sitter's somewhat downbeat and unsmiling pose, summons an atmosphere that jars with the uniform's parade-ground panache – an effect which, again, prefigures the *Bathers*, with its unsmiling seated youths. The 'Brest' sketchbook is sometimes cited as evidence, too, of Seurat's interest in the teachings of the chemist and colour theorist Michel-Eugène Chevreul, of whom he'd been aware thanks to the writings of the aesthetician Charles Blanc, since his days at Lequien's school, as early as 1876. Seurat copied passages from Chevreul's influential book

The Principles of Harmony and Contrast of Colours (1839), which, filled with charts and diagrams, studied the effects of adjacent colours. Seurat's sketch of the fencing soldier, for instance, appears to reflect Chevreul's lessons regarding colour opposites: those trousers are bound, on the right of each leg, by strokes of green, which, on Chevreul's 'chromatic circle', or colour wheel, is opposite its complementary (red). In a famous letter discussing his artistic development, dated 20 June 1890 and addressed to an early supporter, the art critic Félix Fénéon, Seurat characterised the years between 1876 and 1884 as spent 'searching for an optical formula', guided by Blanc, who taught him about 'Chevreul's laws' and (as we shall see) the Romantic artist, and great antagonist of Ingres, Eugène Delacroix.[11] This letter was designed to bolster Seurat's assertion that he, rather than his friend, the painter Paul Signac (whom he'd met, with the breakaway Artistes Indépendants, in 1884), had initiated Neo-Impressionism – a term that Fénéon used for the first time in his article 'The Impressionists in 1886'. In recent years, art historians have downplayed Seurat's dependence on the 'laws' of Chevreul and other theorists: imagination, they argue, as much as intellect, defined his art.

Following his discharge from military service at the end of 1880, Seurat returned to Paris. However, for reasons that remain undocumented, he didn't go back to the Ecole des Beaux-Arts. Instead, during 1881 he started working alongside Aman-Jean in a studio that his friend was renting on the rue de l'Arbalète (a working-class area, in the fifth arrondissement, where many artists and students lived), and created his first independent paintings and works on paper. Most of Seurat's astonishing drawings in Conté crayon (a less crumbly medium than charcoal), which emphasise tone rather than line and often depict anonymous, spectral-looking characters encountered on Paris's streets and in its parks, date from this period. Seurat sometimes worked on them by candlelight.

Together, he and Aman-Jean immersed themselves in the progressive art that the capital had to offer, including work by the Impressionists, who were still exhibiting regularly as a group. Since 1874, when the First Impressionist Exhibition had been held, these artists – including Claude Monet, Camille Pissarro, Pierre-Auguste Renoir (fig. 13) and Degas – had emerged as challengers to the French art establishment. By the time that Seurat became aware of them, they were notorious for rapid, visible brushwork, for the fact that they often began (and sometimes completed) paintings outdoors, and for their resolute focus on modern subject matter, especially the pleasure-seeking pastimes

13 Pierre-Auguste Renoir (1841–1919)
The Skiff '(La Yole)', 1875
Oil on canvas, 71 × 92 cm
The National Gallery, London

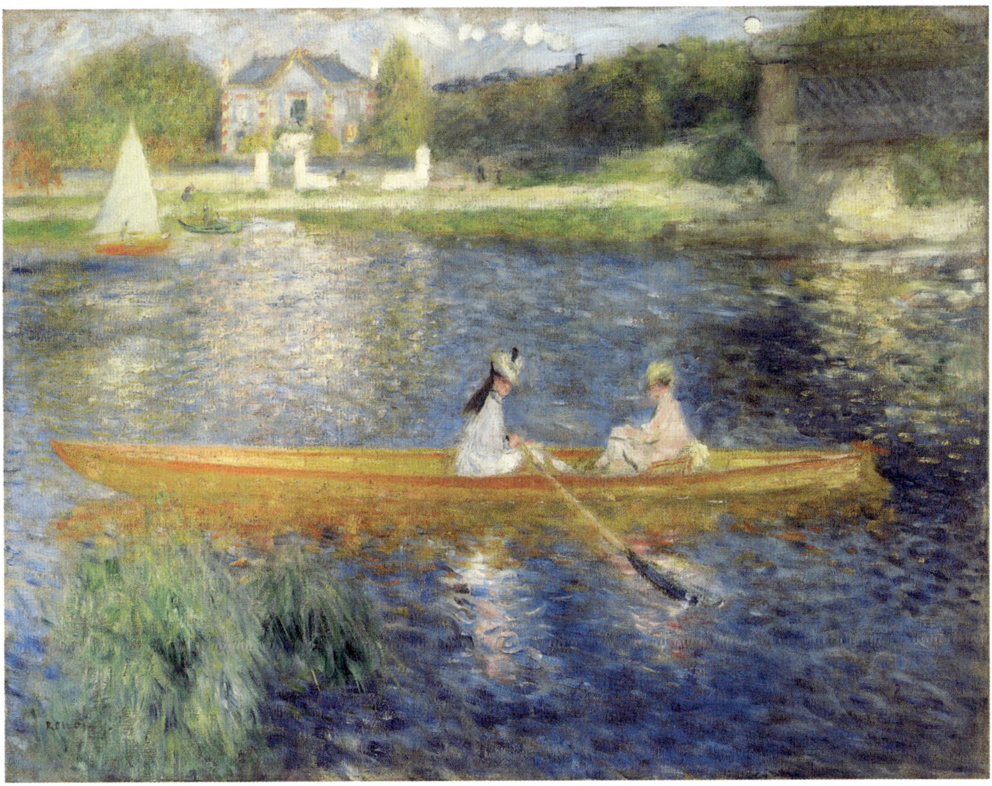

14 *The Anglers*, 1883 (study for *La Grande Jatte*)
Oil on wood, 16 × 25 cm
Musée d'art moderne, Troyes
Donation Pierre et Denise Lévy, 1975

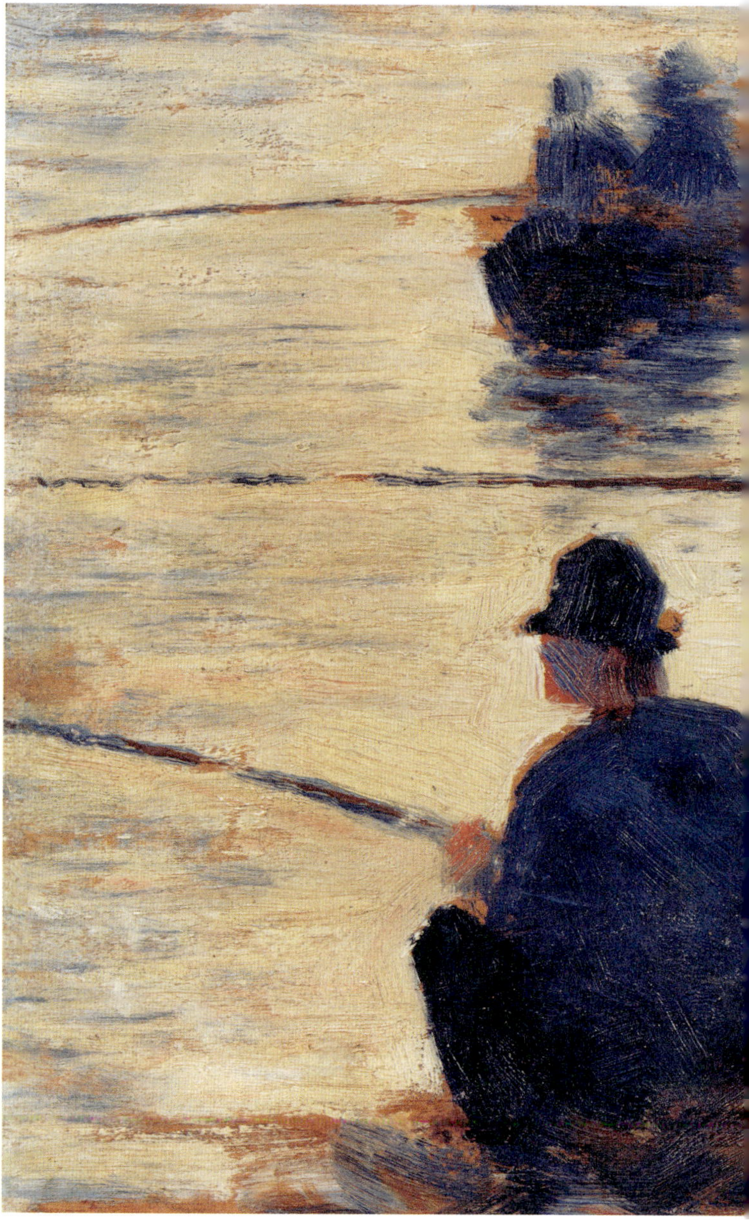

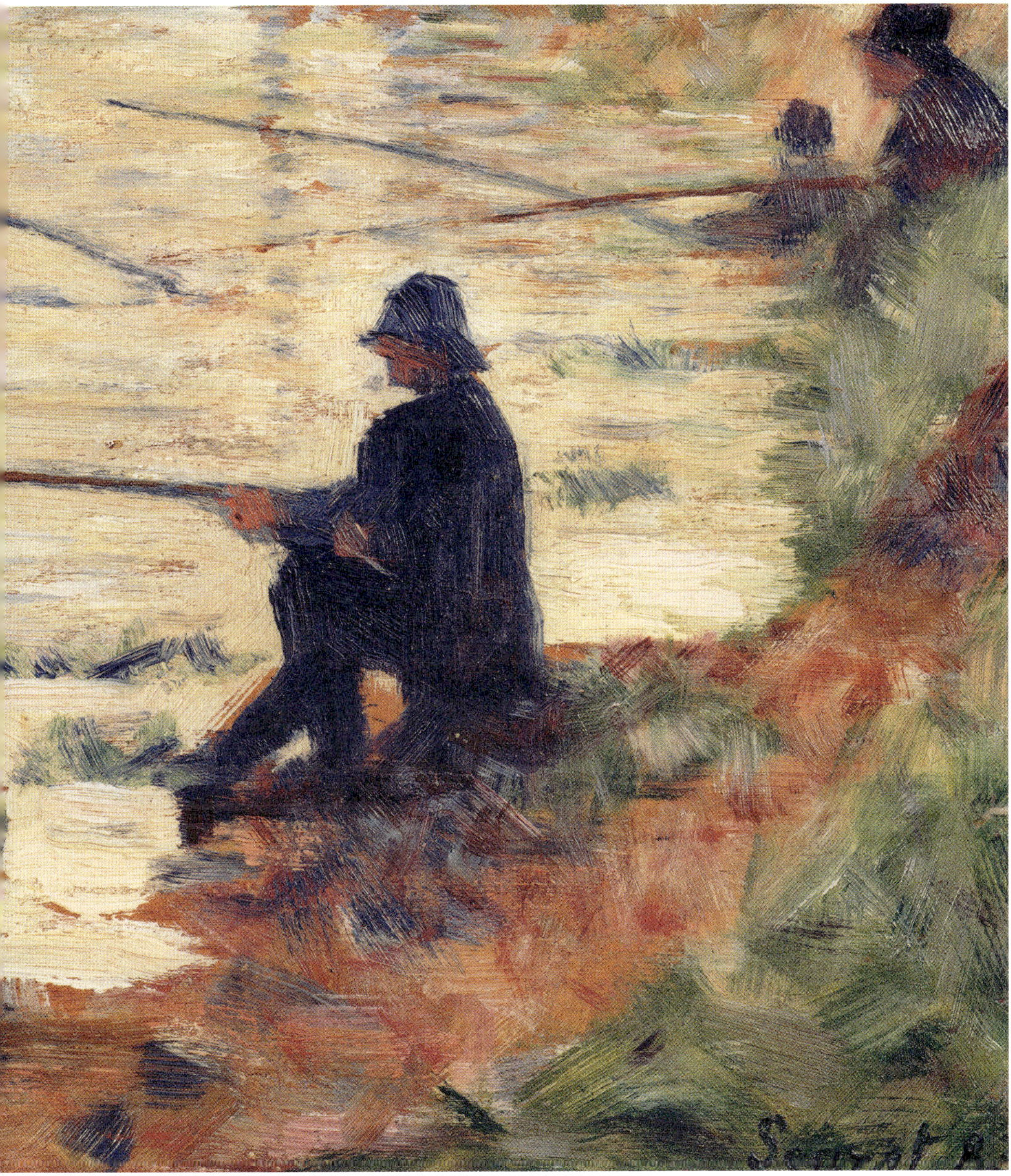

of contemporary bourgeois life. Their impact upon the young Seurat is perhaps most visible in his many paintings from the early 1880s on small wooden (mostly mahogany or walnut) panels (fig. 14), which he often created in the open air, in the manner of the Impressionists, and called *croquetons* ('sketchettes', or little sketches) – a word he possibly invented, derived from the academic term for a swift sketch (*croquis*).

At the same time, Seurat's *croquetons* – which, for modern viewers, hold considerable appeal – are often linked to landscapes by an earlier (and informal) group of French painters known as the Barbizon School, whose numbers included Théodore Rousseau and Jean-François Millet. Inspired by the example of *The Hay Wain* by the British landscapist John Constable, which had been exhibited, to applause, at the Salon of 1824 (and is now a cornerstone of the National Gallery's collection), the Barbizon artists valued naturalism and rural settings. They also painted outside, years before the Impressionists, and favoured a freer, more painterly technique than that taught at the Ecole des Beaux-Arts. In many of his *croquetons*, Seurat deliberately left patches of the wooden ground exposed. This was a little trick he could have picked up while studying pictures by either the Impressionists or the Barbizon artists; in October 1883, i.e., after he'd begun the *Bathers* (which draws on this mid-nineteenth-century tradition of depicting everyday scenes in an un-idealised manner), he even visited the village of Barbizon near the Forest of Fontainebleau with Aman-Jean. They stayed, as the avant-garde had done before them, at the Auberge Ganne. It isn't necessarily the case, therefore, as art historians used to believe, that Seurat's fascination with the Impressionists superseded an earlier interest in the Barbizon painters.

There were other significant influences on Seurat's artistic development. He was fascinated by Delacroix, a brilliant colourist who achieved complex, seemingly vibrating chromatic effects by applying his hues in

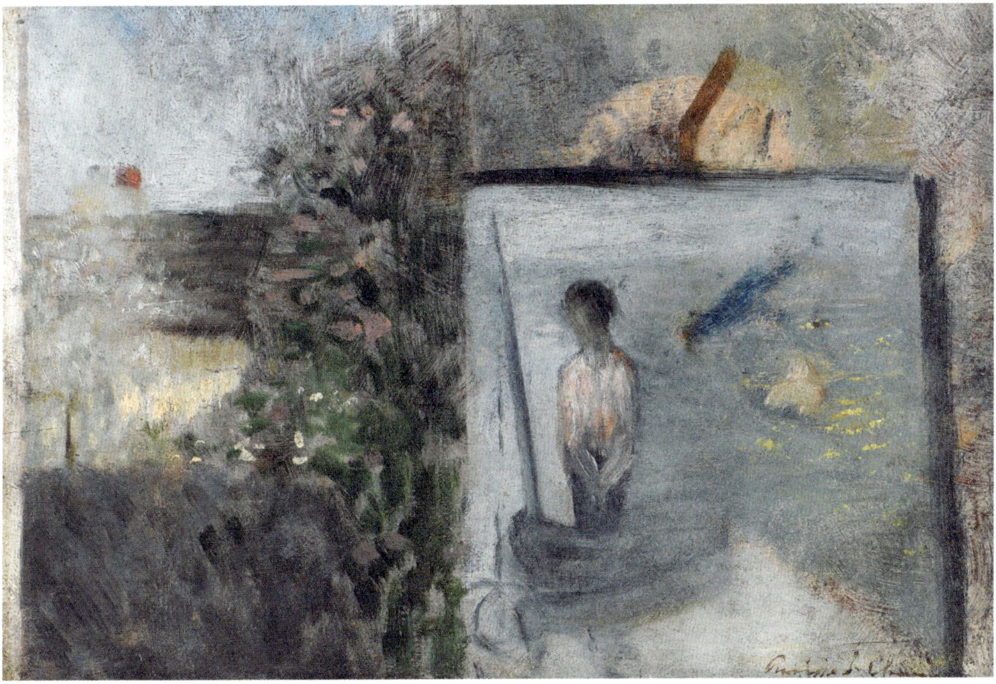

15 *Landscape with 'The Poor Fisherman' by Puvis de Chavannes*, 1881
Oil on wood, 16 × 25 cm
Musée d'Orsay, Paris

a deliberately broken fashion, so that colours were separated into tints. According to one early biographer, Seurat and Aman-Jean, when they were young painters, often visited the Chapel of the Holy Angels in the church of Saint-Sulpice, Paris, 'where they were mesmerised by the spirited frescoes of Delacroix' (as the Impressionists had been as well).[12] Perhaps, then, Seurat's unorthodox approach to colour owed as much to Delacroix's oeuvre as it did to the teachings of Chevreul (even if Delacroix himself was conscious of the chemist's theories). And, in 1881, Seurat made a loose copy (fig. 15) of a painting by the classicising artist Pierre Puvis de Chavannes, on the reverse of a panel depicting a landscape at Saint-Ouen, an industrial district to the north of Paris. Puvis's work, which depicts

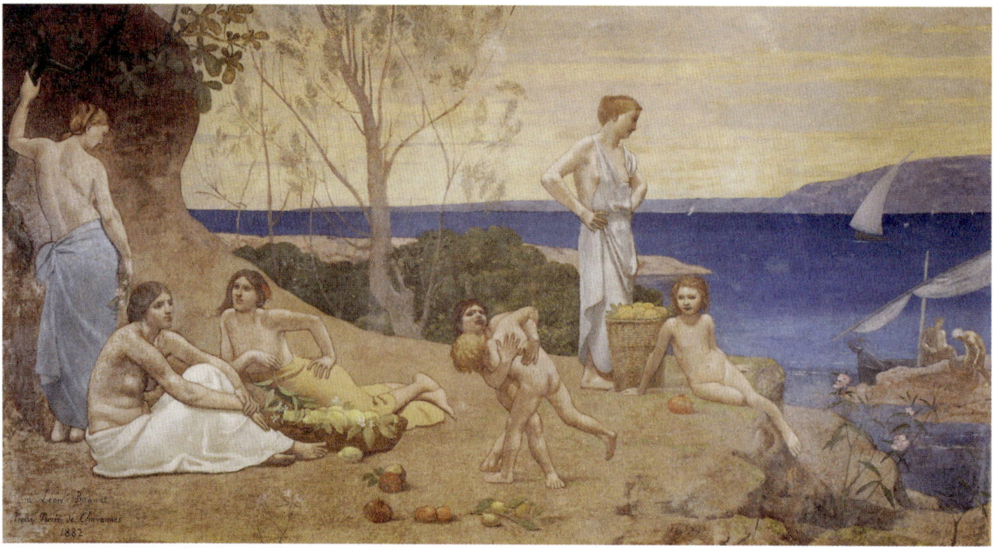

a fisherman standing forlornly in a boat, had appeared at that spring's Salon (and now hangs in the Musée d'Orsay in Paris: *The Poor Fisherman*, 1881).

While Puvis is no longer so familiar today, during his lifetime he won acclaim for his mural cycles decorating civic buildings throughout France and was lauded by Seurat's peers as a paragon of contemporary art. This is likely because the archaic simplicity of his approach irked their Beaux-Arts teachers. Aman-Jean and Seurat may even have assisted Puvis in his Place Pigalle studio, although it has been suggested that Seurat's attitude to the older artist was ambivalent: his drab approximation of Puvis's *pauvre pêcheur* was possibly intended as a take-down.[13] Still, several art historians have sensed a relationship between the *Bathers* and another large oil painting by Puvis, *Pleasant Land* (fig. 16), which was exhibited at the 1882 Salon. Both works feature a series of statuesque, unclothed figures, seemingly lost in reverie, arranged within a composition

16 Pierre Puvis de Chavannes (1824–1898)
Pleasant Land, 1881–2
Oil on canvas, 230 × 300 cm
Musée Bonnat-Helleu, Bayonne

divided between land on the left and water on the right. This parallel helps us to unravel Paul Alexis's perplexed description of the *Bathers*, in his review of the 1884 exhibition organised by the Artistes Indépendants, as a 'fake Puvis de Chavannes'. But we are jumping ahead. In 1882, Seurat started renting his own studio (with a fireplace, no less) on the rue de Chabrol, not far from his mother's apartment, and it was here, in the spring or summer of 1883, that he began *Bathers at Asnières*.

AN EXPANDING CITY

By the early 1880s, Seurat was on the hunt for subject matter, and, when he wasn't looking at pictures by other artists, he spent much of his time exploring the northern suburbs of Paris. During the nineteenth century the city had expanded rapidly. The population, about one million in 1850, had doubled by 1877. Many of the inner suburbs that had earlier attracted the Impressionists – who depicted these semi-rural locales as sites of bourgeois entertainment, where well-heeled city-dwellers could kick back by fishing, picnicking or boating on the river Seine – had grown more commercial and industrial. The demographics of those who frequented the areas had shifted, too.

Asnières, to the north-west of the city, where Monet and his fellow Impressionist Alfred Sisley had often painted, was typical of this trend. Following the construction in 1837 of an iron railway bridge linking Paris with the river port of Le Pecq (fig. 17, the same bridge that's visible in the background of Seurat's *Bathers*), Asnières had become an easy destination for off-duty urbanites looking to relax in a rustic setting, beside or on the water. In the mid-1880s, it still had a reputation as a place for boating, with all the amenities – cafés and restaurants, shops and inns – that day-trippers could need.[14] But its population was growing and changing, as workers moved in to service the railway workshops and the factories of luxury-goods firms such as

Louis Vuitton, which, since 1860, had manufactured luggage in this increasingly industrial district. In Seurat's *Bathers*, the factories and gasworks of Clichy, on the opposite bank, are apparent beyond the bridges (for there are, in fact, two spanning the river in parallel: one supporting the rail track, the other a highway). As a result, by the 1880s there were fewer regattas at Asnières than in the past; to entice their middle-class clientele, the businesses associated with boating had moved further out to places like Argenteuil. By the time that Seurat decided to make Asnières the setting for his first large painting – a setting to which the picture's title directed attention – it had become a sort of in-between zone: neither rural nor urban. Not exclusively bourgeois but, at the same time, hardly shabby. Evidently, the plain, indeterminate character of Asnières (fig. 18) fascinated Seurat, perhaps because it felt different to the prettier suburbs commonly portrayed by other modern painters.

The exact spot he chose for his painting was an area of sloping open ground with a busy towpath known as the

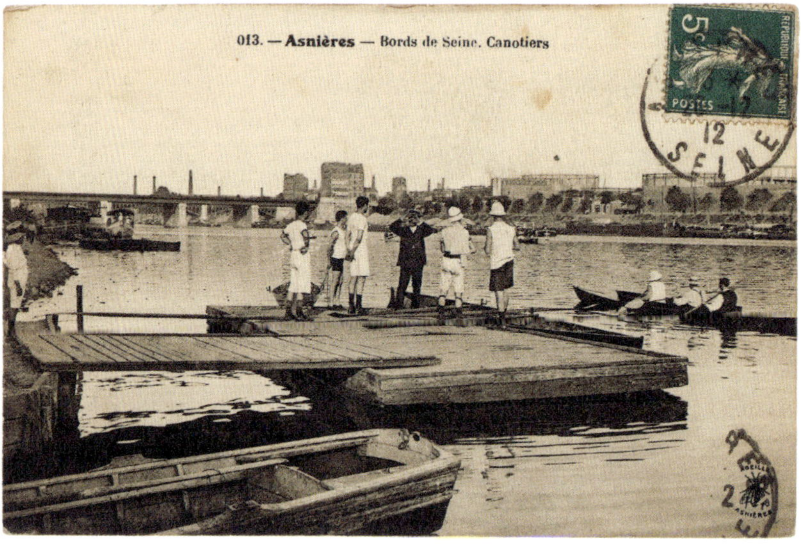

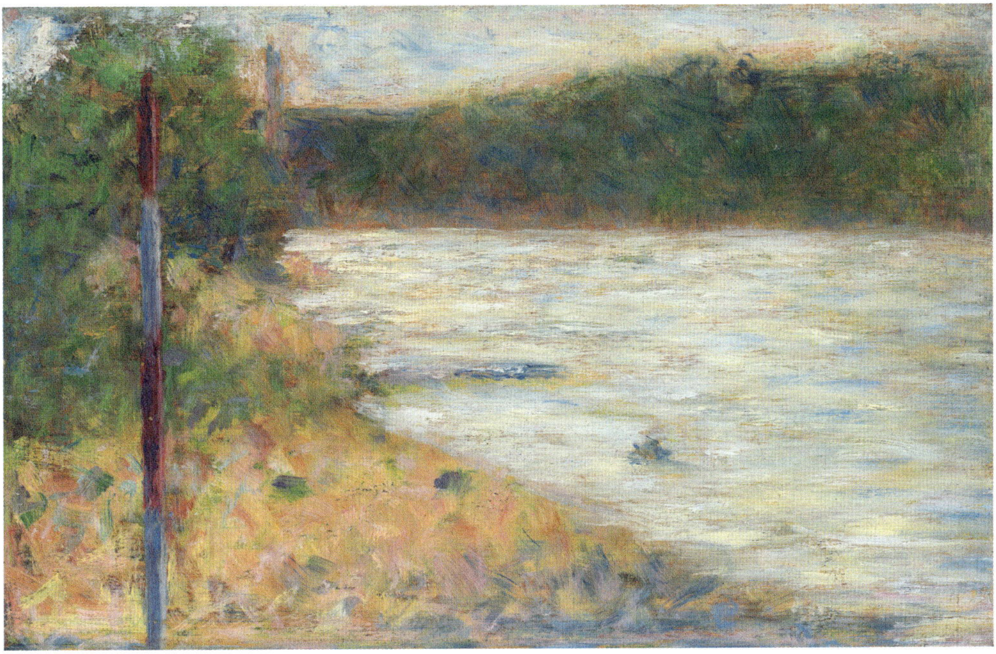

17 Postcard (pre-1912) showing male bathers. The two Asnières bridges are just visible in the background (railway bridge in foreground, road bridge behind). Musée Carnavalet, Histoire de Paris

18 *A River Bank (The Seine at Asnières)*, about 1883
Oil on wood, 15.8 × 24.7 cm
The National Gallery, London

Côte des Ajoux, with an eastward view across the Seine. The dark, bosky foliage in the painting's upper-right corner – with its surreal, conical tree that seems to tilt, at an alarming angle, away from the white sail of a passing boat, which echoes its form in reverse – represents the tip of the elongated island of La Grande Jatte, where, along with restaurants and dancing establishments, parks lured middle-class Parisians to take the air while dressed in up-to-the-minute fashions. One of these, on the island's north-west shore, would be the setting for Seurat's second major canvas: *A Sunday on La Grande Jatte – 1884* (see fig. 29). Although in the *Bathers* Seurat artfully edited out many of the conspicuous suburban buildings along the embankment at Asnières, he retained, on its left, a small sandy ravine seemingly gouged out of the riverbank. Like the mysteriously slanting, off-kilter tree on La Grande Jatte, its stretched-out, triangular void rhymes with the outline of the far-off sail on the other side of the river. This gully was used not only to launch or land small boats but also to lead horses into the river, where they could be bathed and watered. According to the American art historian and Seurat specialist Robert L. Herbert, the word *baignade*, which the artist included in the painting's original title, was printed on old maps to designate sites along the Seine where, for a small fee, dogs and horses would be washed by local boys.[15] It didn't signify a charming bathing spot where members of the public could enjoy some downtime, but carried working-class connotations.

Horses appear in four of the panels that Seurat painted while planning his composition. In one (fig. 19), a white horse ridden bareback by a youth in orange underwear stands a few feet out in the river, so that the water's surface grazes its belly. In the same picture, a dark brown horse closer to shore is being patted – or washed – by a figure dressed in a white shirt. In total, there are 13 oil studies for the *Bathers*, all on wooden panels, along with around 10 preliminary crayon drawings, with

19 *Horses in the Water*, about 1883 (study for *Bathers at Asnières*)
Oil on panel, 15.2 × 24.8 cm
Private collection
On extended loan to the Courtauld, London

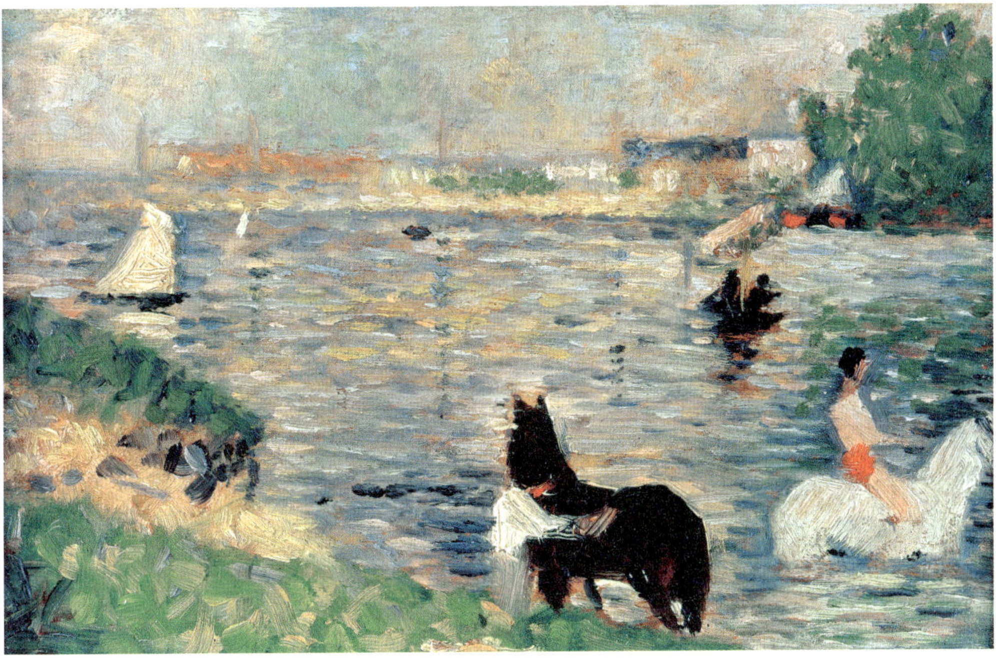

characteristically velvety blacks. Here, perhaps, we may detect the legacy of Seurat's Beaux-Arts training, which inculcated the importance of painstaking preparation before embarking on a large composition; in a letter to Signac written in the late summer of 1888, Pissarro carped that Seurat 'comes from the Ecole des Beaux-Arts, he's impregnated with it'.[16] It's impossible to arrange these studies, in which Seurat experimented with various ideas, in a definitive sequence. It's tempting to assume that the *croquetons* came first, because several have an open-air quality, as if painted on-site; and that the drawings must have followed, since they were demonstrably executed in the studio. (An easel is visible, for instance, in the background of the 1882–3 study *Boy Viewed from Behind*.) This would reinforce the idea of Seurat the methodical artist, mechanically progressing from initial idea to finished canvas. It's more likely, though, as some art historians have suggested, that he worked on the oil studies and drawings simultaneously – returning to Asnières to record fresh impressions as the need arose.[18]

In the oils, Seurat subtly plays with the view from his chosen vantage point. At times, he removes figures altogether, as if, like a theatre director, he wished to establish the lineaments of his set. He also tries out different groupings: in one panel, a rainbow appears above three clothed figures who sit apart (fig. 20). Some ideas (the horses, the rainbow) were jettisoned, but, gradually, various elements found in the finished painting coalesced: bathers in water; a prominent seated figure to the left; crumpled clothing on the grass; factories belching out smoke; a round-shouldered, seated bather commanding the composition. The Art Institute of Chicago owns what is thought to be the final study for the *Bathers* (fig. 21), but, while its design is like that of the finished picture, it isn't identical: the red hat worn by the bather at the right edge, for instance, has a wider brim. Due to its more vigorous brushwork, the mood of the Chicago study is less sombre, too. This is further evidence that Seurat wasn't an artistic automaton replicating what he'd already worked out.

The drawings – carefully executed in Conté crayon on high-quality, prominently ridged sheets of milky-white laid paper produced by the company Michallet, which Seurat often used – are much closer to the finished painting, as the artist resolves poses and nuances of tone. A still life (*Hat, Shoes and Undergarments: Study for 'Bathers at Asnières'*, 1883–4, Fogg Art Museum) even focuses on the discarded clothing in the foreground of the final work. Seurat seems less concerned, in the drawings, with recording his models' particularities. Rather, these sheets suggest that he was striving for strong, simplified, semi-idealised and abstracted forms, characterised by interlocking geometric shapes, as well as a complex interplay between light and dark. In the Conté-crayon study for the central seated bather (fig. 22), Seurat creates an effect – sometimes described as 'irradiation' – that we often find in his drawings, by contrasting the darker, shaded areas of the boy's head, neck and spine with a glowing penumbra in the background. On the other side of the figure this is reversed, as the edges of his illuminated right shoulder, biceps and forearm meet darkness, so that they stand out. In the finished painting, a bright, silvery (and non-naturalistic) strip of water appears to caress the same bather's back and shoulders and cosset the profile of his face, while the patch of river beyond his right shoulder and arm is, abruptly, a much deeper shade of blue. As well as helping to define his form, this gives him a sort of halo – suggesting, perhaps, a spiritual significance to this seemingly mundane scene. If Seurat's *Bathers* hints at quiet revelation, it seems to do so thanks in part to this radiance, which functions a little like that well-worn modern trope for inspiration: an illuminated light bulb. What, though, is this brooding bather thinking?

20 *The Rainbow*, 1883
(study for *Bathers at Asnières*)
Oil on wood, 15.5 × 24.5 cm
The National Gallery, London

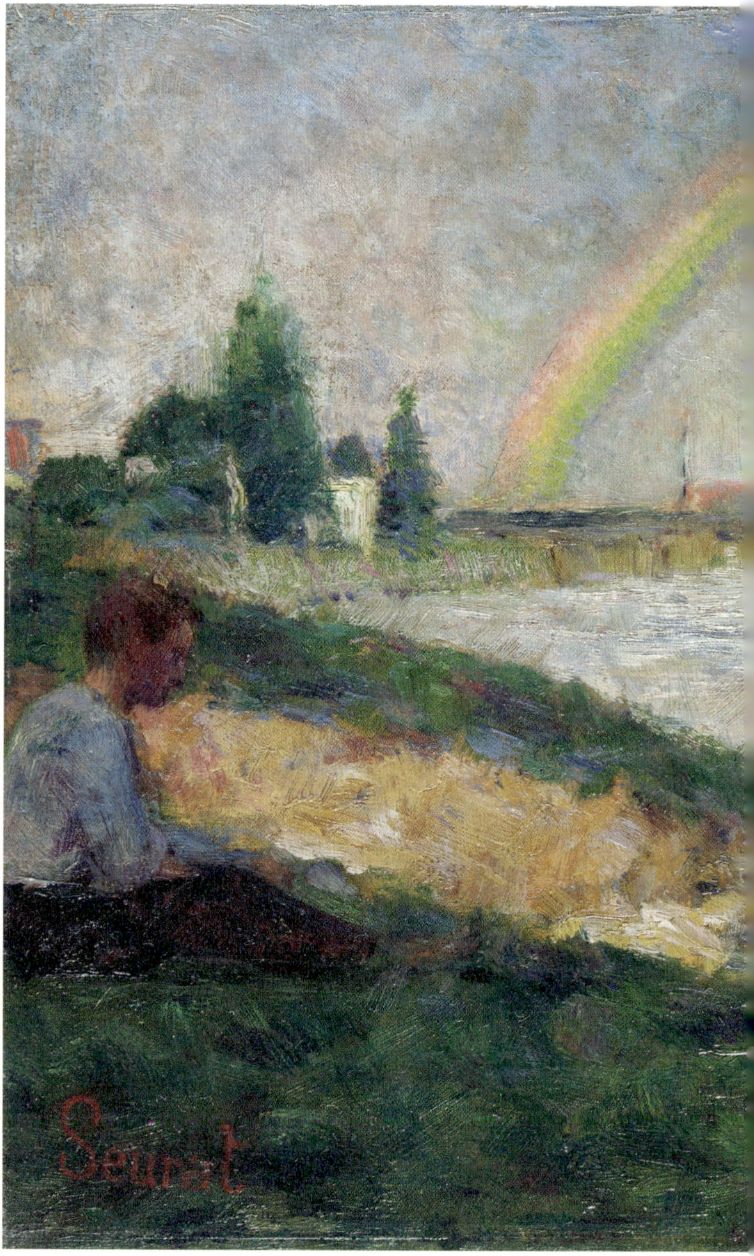

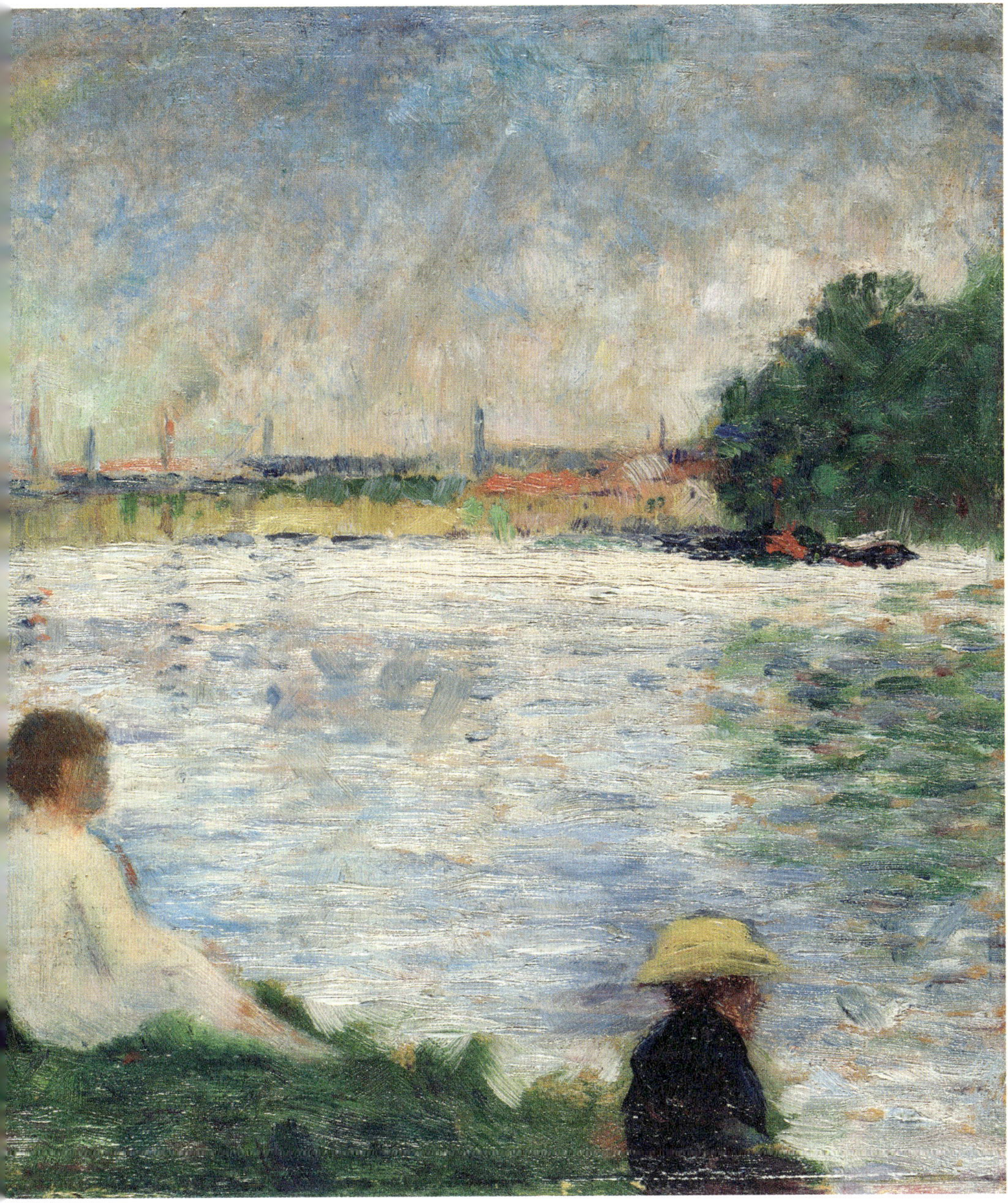

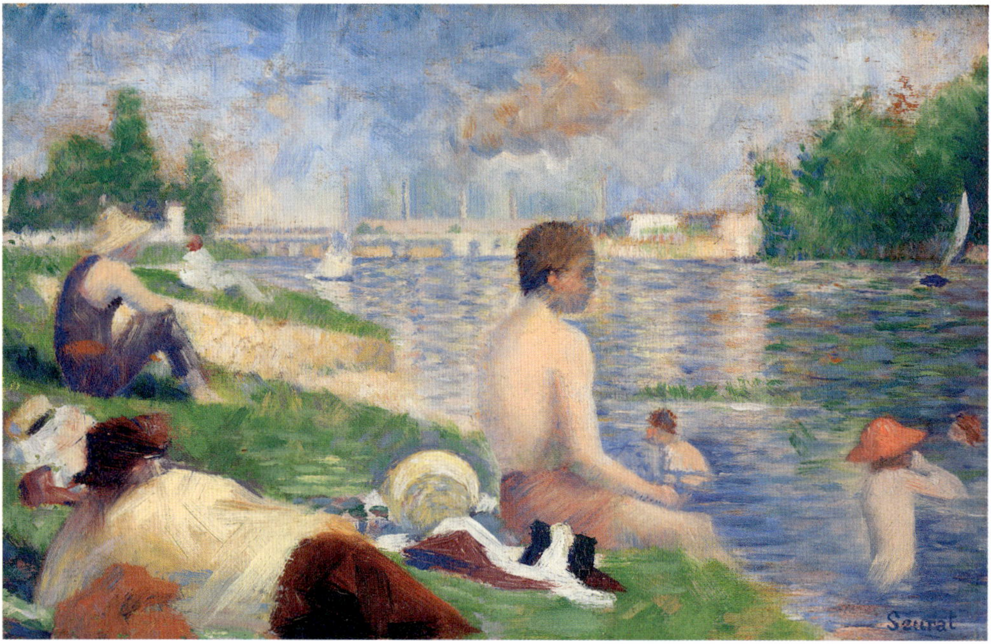

21 *Final study for 'Bathers at Asnières'*, 1883
Oil on panel, 15.8 × 25.1 cm
Art Institute of Chicago
Gift of the Adele R. Levy Fund, Inc.

22 *Seated Nude*, 1883
(study for *Bathers at Asnières*)
Conté crayon on cream paper, 31.7 × 24.7 cm
National Galleries of Scotland, Edinburgh. Purchased by Private Treaty 1982

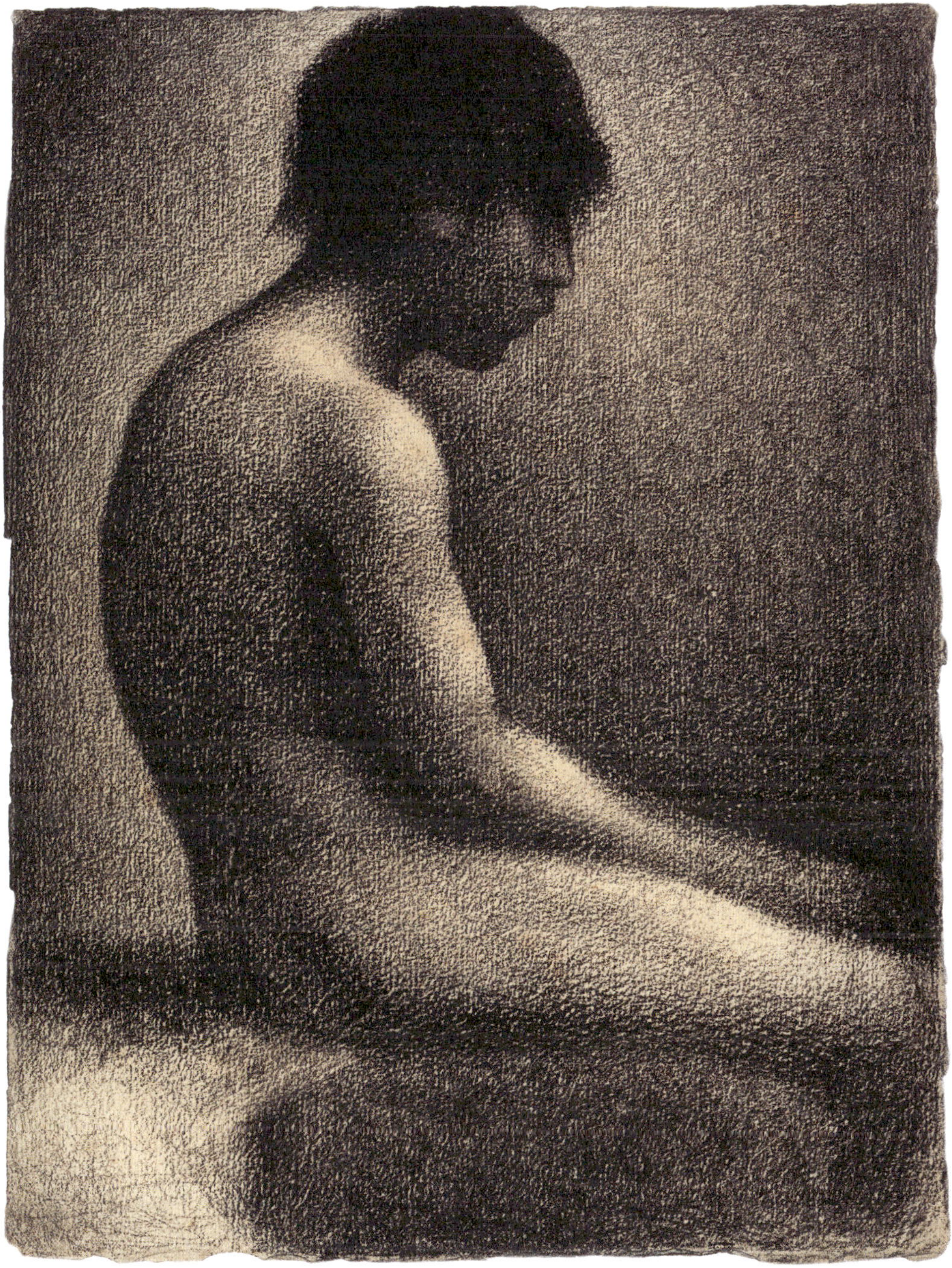

THE ISOLATION OF MODERN LIFE

Understanding the context from which the *Bathers* emerged informs our interpretation of this enigmatic picture. But the more one returns to scrutinise it, the more complex – and, seemingly, contradictory – it becomes. Consider its relationship with the sort of art routinely exhibited during the nineteenth century at the Salon (where, as we know, Seurat hoped it would be shown). In various ways, the *Bathers* apes a typical Salon picture. It's big, with the heft of something you might find in a museum. Its composition is harmonious and was worked up following a period of careful preparation, involving many studies, by an emerging artist steeped in Beaux-Arts traditions.

The motif of the male bather has a long pedigree in Western art, stretching back to the Renaissance.[18] And, like a lot of nineteenth-century Salon paintings, Seurat's *Bathers* invokes the art of antiquity. As a student, Seurat drew ancient sculptures such as the *Ares Borghese* in the Louvre (which, according to friends, he visited, to study); 13 drawings after plaster casts of antique sculptures also survive (fig. 23). The man lying in the foreground of the *Bathers* alludes to classical statues of reclining river gods, such as a famous marble figure from the west pediment of the Parthenon in Athens. Seurat, likely working from a lithograph, drew this figure during his first year at Lequien's school in 1875 (fig. 24). The foreshortened, circular hat also in the painting's foreground might even be a prompt to interpret the central figure as a bathetic reworking of the celebrated classical Greek sculpture of a discus-thrower by the Athenian sculptor Myron, known via several Roman copies. If this feels like a stretch, we can surely agree that the figures in the *Bathers* – who are mostly in profile, and rendered with a curious, relief-like flatness – are arranged, quite deliberately, in the manner of an ancient frieze: 'I want to make modern people, in their essential traits, move about as they do on those friezes, and place them on canvases organised by harmonies of colour', Seurat once told Kahn.[19] In short, there are classical components to the *Bathers* (not least its kinship, discussed earlier, with Puvis's *Pleasant Land*).

Yet, as we have seen, the Salon rejected it. And, although we don't know why it did so, it seems reasonable to speculate that the painting unsettled the jury, despite its Beaux-Arts DNA. Unlike a quintessential Salon picture, it has no didactic moral, no narrative that needs to be parsed. It doesn't depict a recognisable moment from history or from the Bible. If anything, Seurat's bathers seem to challenge, rather than perpetuate, the classical tradition of the heroic male nude. The figures don't strut about or perform impressive sporting feats, but lounge languidly, as if waiting for someone else – someone stronger and more physically developed, perhaps – to take centre stage. The modern 'river god' in the foreground isn't a muscle-bound divinity; his torso is, rather, hidden in a shapeless, sack-like white coat. If, in any way, the central bather is in dialogue with ancient statuary, then, surely, this is a sophisticated joke.

If the *Bathers* isn't a Salon picture, perhaps it's an Impressionist one? After all, a couple of years later, in 1886, Seurat presented *La Grande Jatte* (fig. 29), along with three drawings, a panel and four more canvases (including *Le Bec du Hoc, Grandcamp* (fig. 4)), at the eighth and last Impressionist exhibition. Even here, though, we rapidly run into problems. Yes, *Bathers at Asnières* presents a scene of modern life, and, yes, it depicts the artist's contemporaries at leisure – two hallmarks of paradigmatic Impressionist art. In addition, the setting, on the Seine, feels familiar to anyone who's encountered paintings by Monet or Renoir. But the way the paint is handled – what art historians call its 'facture' – is distinctly un-Impressionist. When he wanted to, Seurat could paint in a spontaneous, immediate manner, with broken brushwork and bright colours; several of his *croquetons* bear more than a superficial

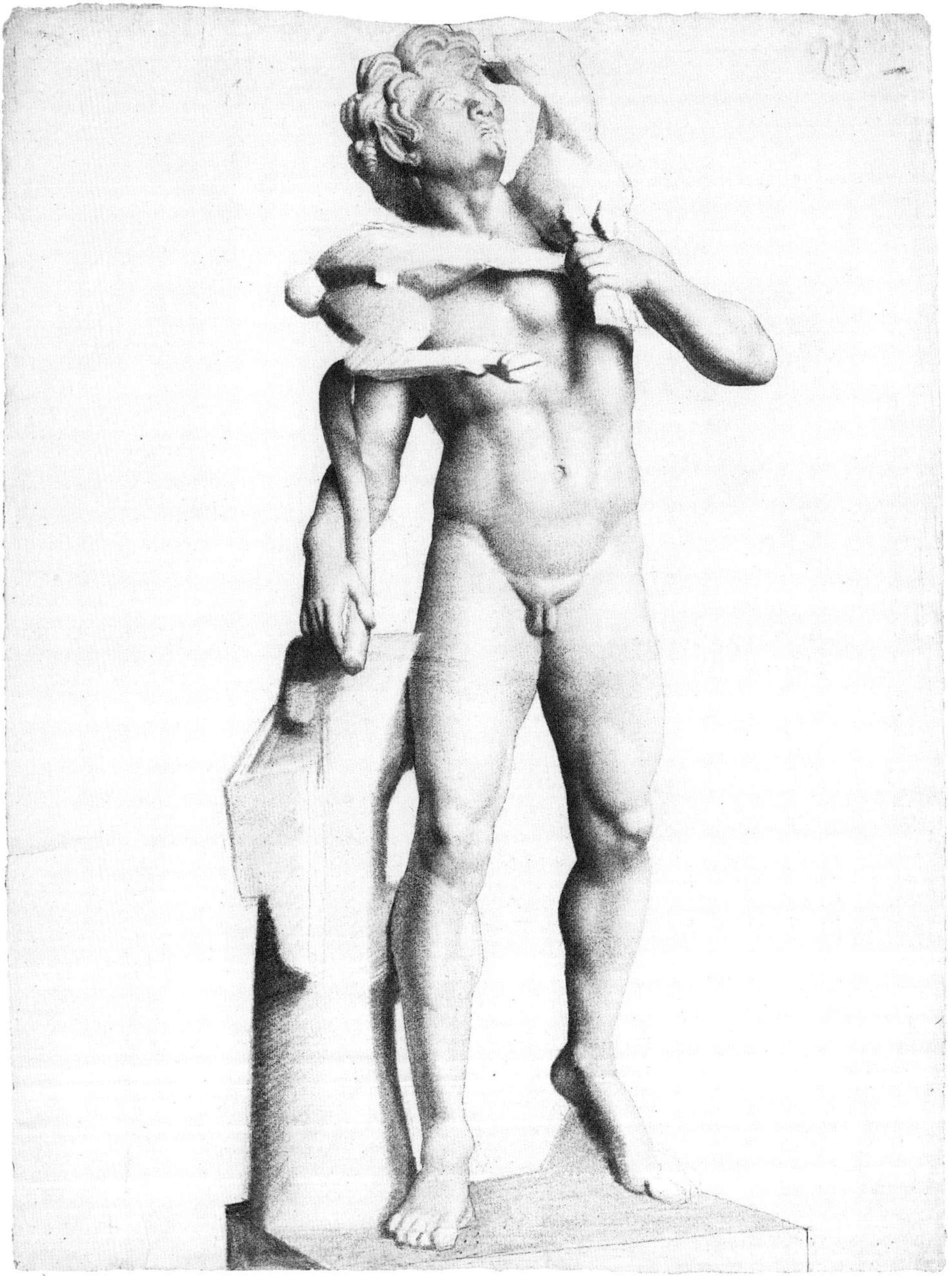

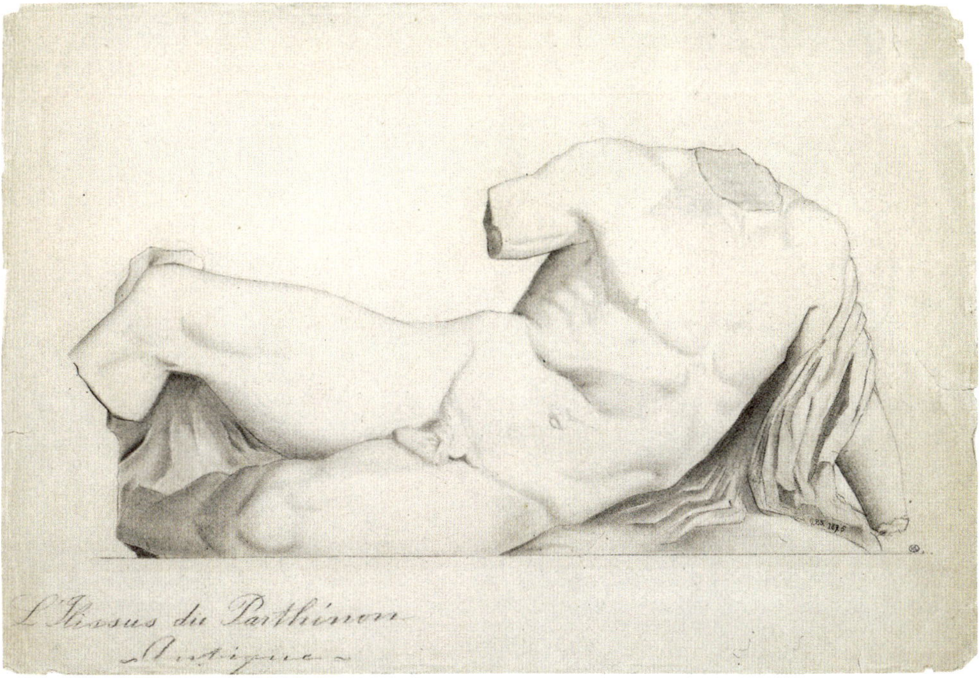

23 *Antique Statue, Satyr with Goat*, 1877–9
Charcoal on paper,
63.5 × 48.3 cm
Private collection, New York

24 *Study of the Ilissus of the Parthenon*, 1875
Pencil, charcoal and smudged charcoal on grey-pink paper,
35.8 × 53.7 cm
Musée du Louvre, Paris

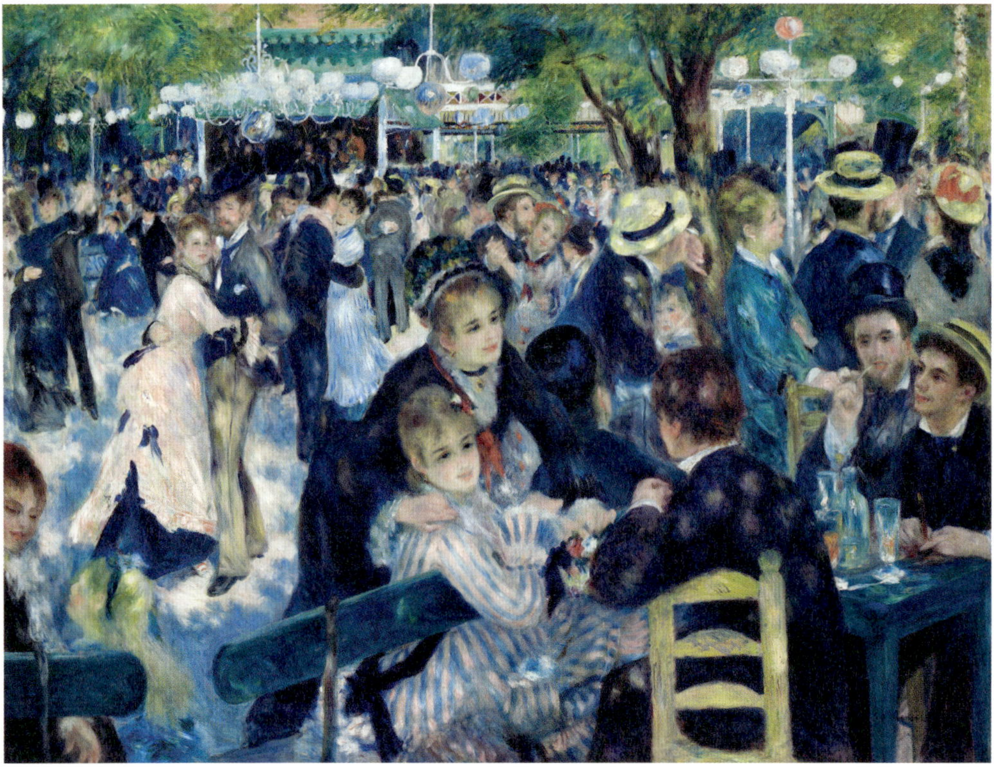

25 Pierre-Auguste Renoir (1841–1919)
Dance at Le Moulin de la Galette, 1876
Oil on canvas, 131.5 × 176.5 cm
Musée d'Orsay, Paris

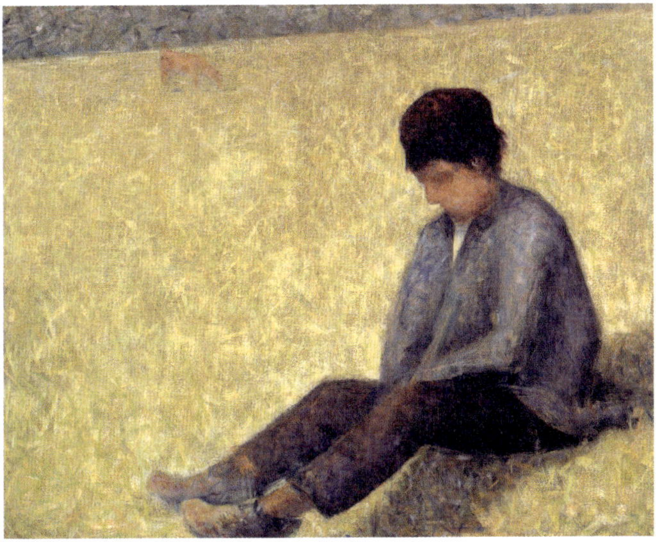

26 *Boy sitting in a Meadow*, about 1882–3
Oil on canvas, 63.5 × 79.6 cm
Kelvingrove Art Gallery and Museum, Glasgow

resemblance to, for instance, Renoir's sunlit, Seine-set *The Skiff* (see fig. 13). Yet, in the *Bathers*, the handling of paint is controlled, chalky and flat. It feels very different to Renoir's scintillating, tremulous touch. For the trees in the background and the grass, Seurat employed a technique known as *balayé*, in which colours are mixed but used dryly, with minimal oil, and applied with hog-hair brushes in short, criss-crossing strokes like chopped straw (*balayé* means, literally, 'broom-swept'). 'Flat', too, could describe the composition's overall mood, which, despite the sunlight, has none of the suave effervescence of Impressionist portrayals of bourgeois high jinks. What do Seurat's stark figures have in common with, say, the sun-dappled, natty socialites and hedonists, dripping with money and bonhomie, in Renoir's *Dance at Le Moulin de la Galette* (fig. 25)? Not much. They are, seemingly, 'have-nots' –

unlike those ritzy 'haves' in the *Bathers'* background, being ferried to a desirable destination (perhaps La Grande Jatte, where that public park, subsequently depicted by Seurat, was located). Even in this little boat, though, the atmosphere seems formal: the affluent couple sits upright, ramrod-straight and primly apart, while the tricolour remains rolled up.

To what class, then, if not the *haute bourgeoisie*, do these men belong? Their clothes, like the transitional setting of Asnières, are ambiguous: they could be proletarian workers or artisans or petit-bourgeois professionals. It isn't clear. The bowler hat worn by the man lolling in the foreground isn't working-class apparel, but the seated figure on the left, sporting that pink sash and loose-fitting trousers, is dressed in a traditional carpenter's or boat-builder's outfit. Here, it's worth noting that many of Seurat's more modest paintings of the early 1880s (fig. 26) depict workers such as stone breakers, gardeners and peasants (suggesting that, at this stage in his career, he wished to emulate Millet's portrayals of impoverished rural folk). If anything, then, the *Bathers* feels like a reaction against Impressionism. There's a slower rhythm to the painting – a sense, even, that Impressionism's whirligig has come to a stop.

With hindsight, we perceive that the artist who conceived this artwork must have been on the same wavelength as Cezanne, who painted his own series of bathers towards the end of his life (fig. 27), and once said that his ambition was to 'make of Impressionism something solid and durable like the art of museums' – which is as good a definition as you'll find of what art historians call Post-Impressionism.[20] Solid, durable: these adjectives fit the *Bathers*, which is painstakingly constructed, in an almost abstract manner, from elements that form corresponding geometric shapes: various uprights, for instance, such as the bridges' supports and those factory chimneys, offset the grand diagonal that

27 Paul Cezanne (1839–1906). *Bathers (Les Grandes Baigneuses),* about 1894–1905
Oil on canvas, 127.2 × 196.1 cm
The National Gallery, London

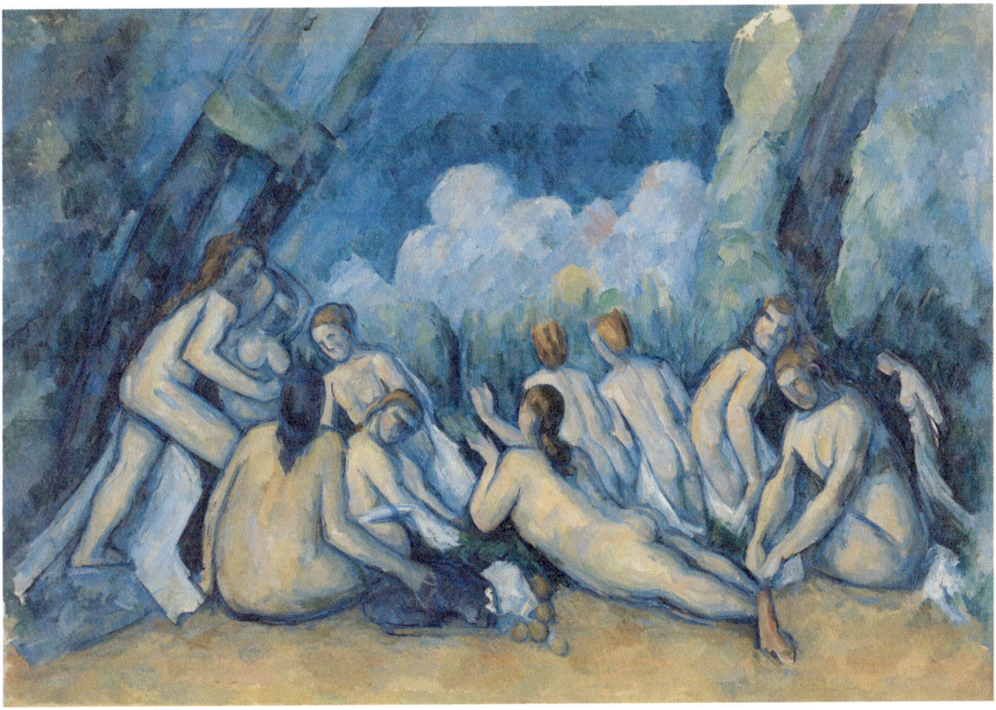

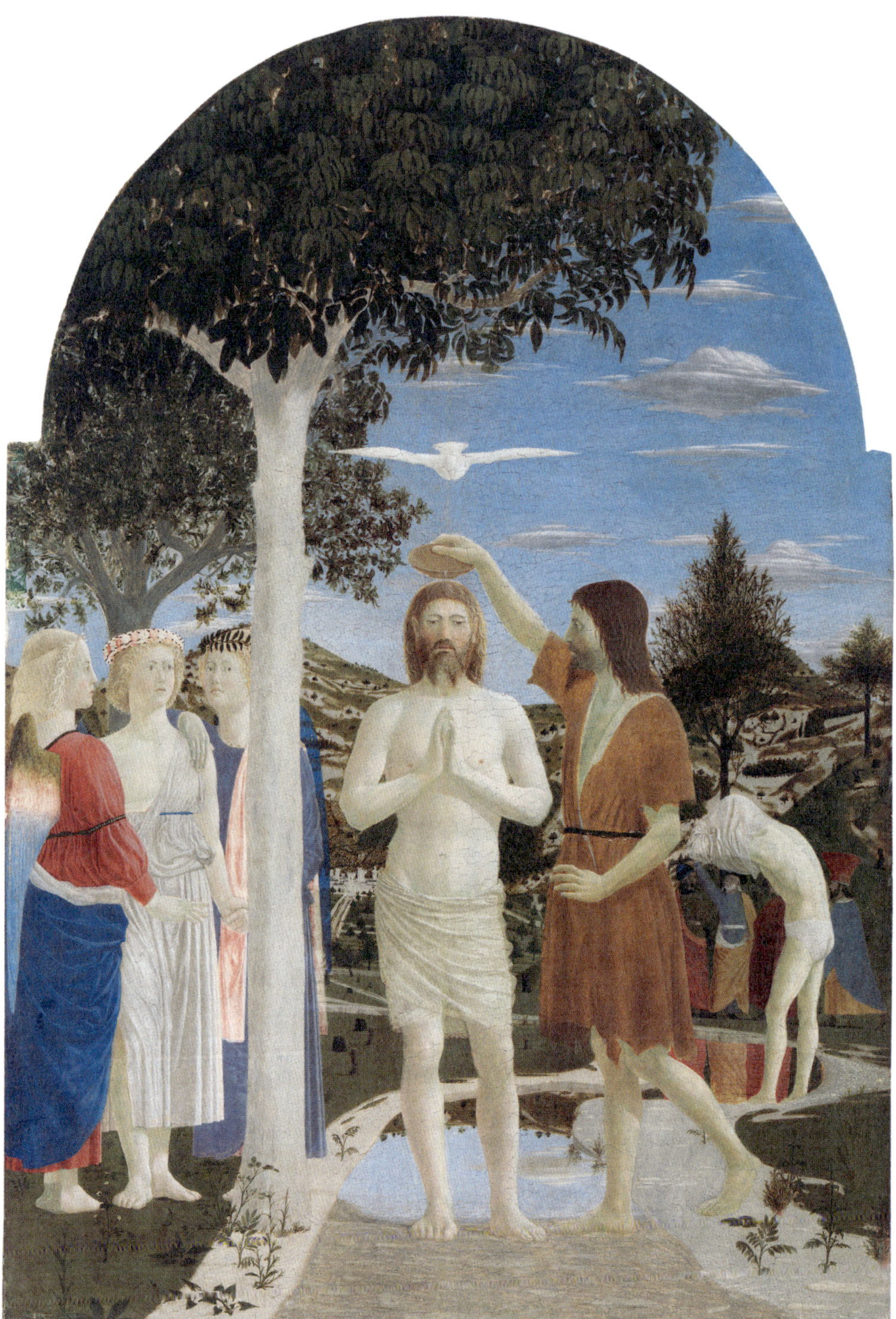

28 Piero della Francesca (about 1415/20–1492)
The Baptism of Christ, about 1437–45
Egg tempera on wood, 167 × 116 cm
The National Gallery, London

bisects the painting into two zones (verdant bank versus river and sky). In 1886, after encountering it in an exhibition organised in New York by the French art dealer Paul Durand-Ruel, an anonymous reviewer compared Seurat's *Bathers* to an 'early [i.e., *quattrocento*, or fifteenth-century] Italian fresco'.[21] It's true, it does share some of the precise, ordered spirit of those nevertheless poetic images by the Italian Renaissance painter (and mathematician) Piero della Francesca, with whom Seurat – with his, as Fry put it, 'mathematical' mind – has been frequently linked.[22] Perhaps there is even an echo within the *Bathers* of the figure in the background of Piero's painting *The Baptism of Christ* (fig. 28) who is undressing to enter the water. For the British artist and critic Michael Ayrton, 'No artist since Raphael has had a surer command of the resources of geometry' than Seurat, who summons, in the *Bathers*, 'a serene poetry of almost puritanical gravity'.[23]

Bathers at Asnières seems to present not a naturalistic depiction of reality, but reality's distillation. Its figures aren't idealised, but nor are they individuals. They're types: frozen, static and apart. To what extent does this reflect Seurat's reserved temperament? Quite a lot, you might suspect. But his bathers don't resonate today because they reveal his personality. Rather, they reverberate because they express something more universally felt: the isolation of modern life. Hence the painting's strangely serious (albeit ordered and tranquil) mood. Seurat may have painted a summer's day – Herbert once described it as 'an allegory of summertime', albeit a highly unusual one – but despite the heat (which has prompted several of its protagonists to undress), there is in the air, as it were, an incongruous chill.[24] In Seurat's vision of leisure, work, as represented by the factory, isn't far away. This idyll, it turns out, isn't all that idyllic.

AFTERLIVES

The Salon des Indépendants, at which *Bathers at Asnières* made its public debut, opened on 15 May 1884. Although the painting received only a few brief notices, the exhibition itself proved pivotal in Seurat's career. While participating in the show (which resulted in the formation, that summer, of the Société des Artistes Indépendants, which still exists), he fraternised with, and befriended, several like-minded young artists, including Angrand and Henri-Edmond Cross, as well as Signac, who also subsequently started separating their colours into little dots. Within a week of the Salon's opening, Seurat was already at work on his next big painting, *A Sunday on La Grande Jatte – 1884* (fig. 29), which, he told Fénéon, he began on Ascension Day (that year, 22 May). Although it was ready for exhibition the following spring, the Salon des Indépendants for which it was earmarked was postponed. It wasn't presented in public until it appeared in the Impressionists' final exhibition, which opened on 15 May 1886. A few months later, it was displayed again, at the second exhibition of the Société des Artistes Indépendants (where it appeared alongside work by Angrand, Cross, Signac and others), which inspired Fénéon to deploy in print the term 'Neo-Impressionist method'. *La Grande Jatte* made Seurat's name – it was even written about in London – and he became known as Impressionism's upstart adversary, reconnecting modernity with tradition. It remains his most famous painting: in 1986, it was featured in a sequence in American filmmaker John Hughes's teen comedy *Ferris Bueller's Day Off*, during which the protagonists, a trio of slackers bunking off high school, mooch around the Art Institute of Chicago. So, unravelling the nature of its relationship with the *Bathers*, with which it has much in common (it may even have been intended as a companion piece), is important.

In this spectacular canvas of comparable dimensions, Seurat, as it were, flips his viewpoint by crossing the Seine and settling on the island of La Grande Jatte. Once again, it's a sunny day, but this time we face a crowd of around fifty people, most of whom are much better dressed than the young men in *Bathers at Asnières*. Here, the figures sit, stand and stroll beneath parasols and the canopies of trees, on and about the river's grassy banks. It's as if we have, by magic, become passengers on the little ferryboat conveying the *Bathers'* well-to-do couple, which has now deposited us somewhere more enticing; it has even been suggested that Seurat added the detail of the ferry, which wasn't part of his original plan for the *Bathers*, after embarking on *La Grande Jatte*, to link the two compositions – which he possibly intended to be shown together.[25] Here, the viewer senses immediately, is a more sophisticated world than that of the *Bathers*, populated by chic Parisians, but also, perhaps, one that's more pretentious, pompous and deceitful; the uncanny 'chill' perceptible in the *Bathers* is still there.

Despite the prominence of several standing figures, who appear as rigid as any represented in ancient Egyptian art (and, along with the tree trunks' uprights, structure the composition), there's a greater sense, in *La Grande Jatte*, of animation. A pug in the foreground, with a delicate white bow attached to its collar, leaps in the direction of another, larger (and unbothered) dog with a black coat, thereby leading the viewer's eye into the *mêlée*. A tawny butterfly flits about in the sunlight. A little girl with flowing hair runs towards a clump of trees that stand like a Greek temple's columned facade in the background. This time, too, there's a pronounced impression of social cohesion. Evidently many of the people arranged in little bunches in the painting know each other, such as the central mother and doll-like child (the only figure who looks directly at the viewer), and the self-regarding couple looming over the foreground. (He puffs on a cigar while his companion, dressed in an extravagant bustle, clutches a delicate chain attached to a pet monkey.) We're now somewhere frequented by both sexes, the old and the young: to the left, a wizened woman too weak to hold her parasol aloft is accompanied by a nurse, who, with her back to us, appears like a cairn of abstract shapes, and may be the only visible worker.

Overleaf:
29 *A Sunday on La Grande Jatte – 1884*, 1884–6
Oil on canvas, 207.5 × 308.1 cm
Art Institute of Chicago. Helen Birch Bartlett Memorial Collection

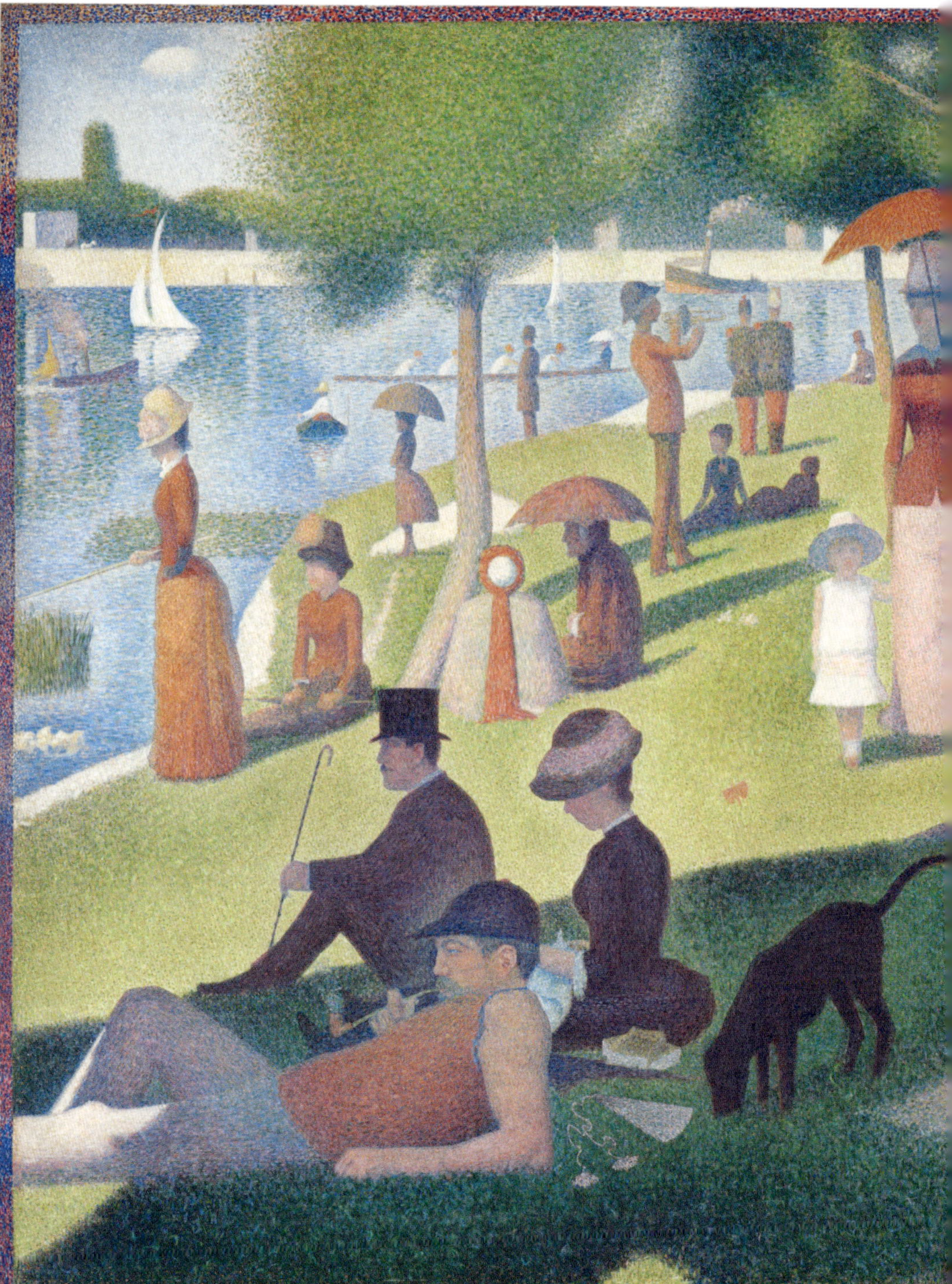

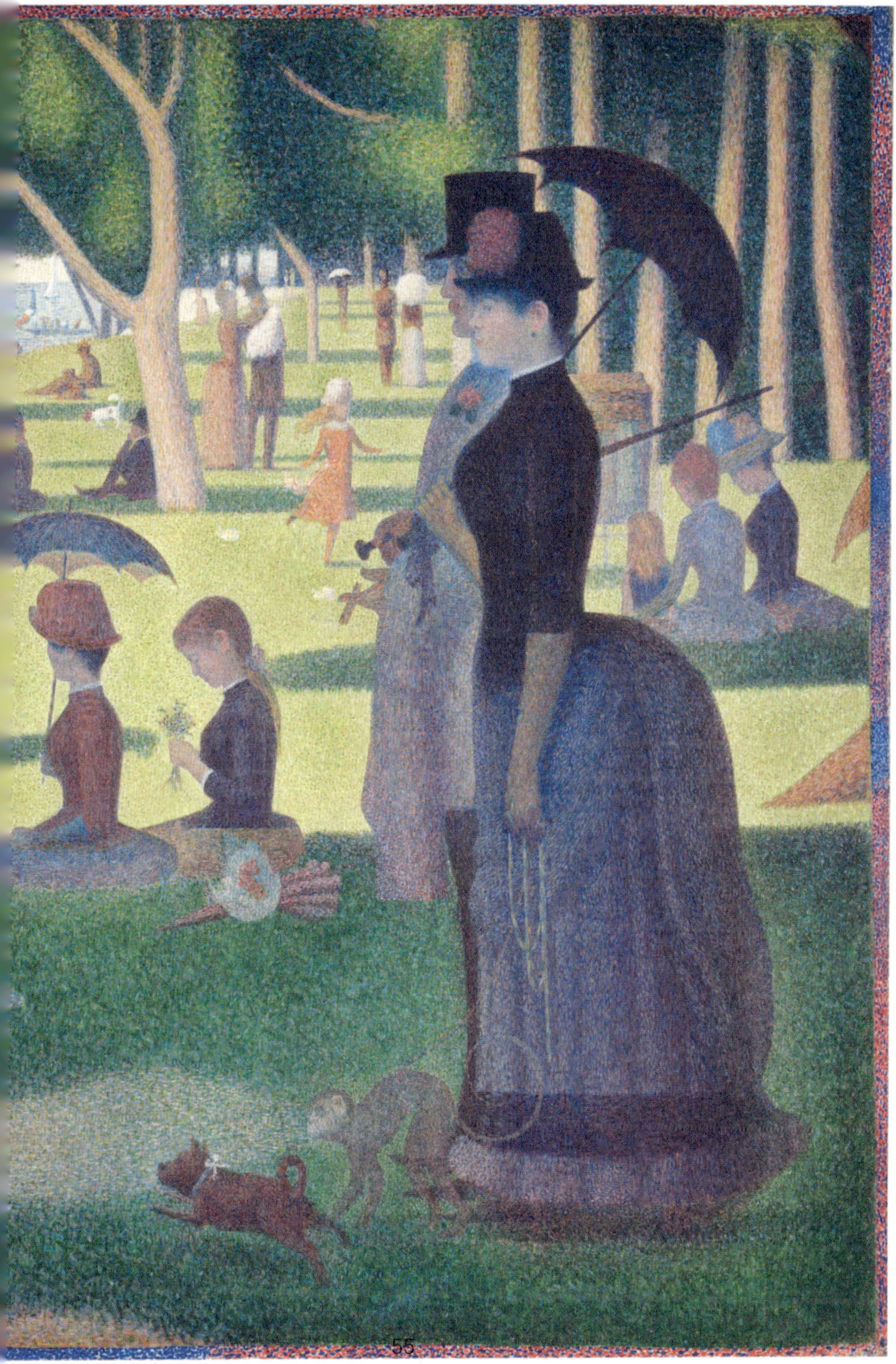

Yet, inadvertently or otherwise, Seurat ensures continuity between this masterpiece and its predecessor, not only by retaining the sunlit setting beside the Seine but also by revisiting and developing various motifs. In the *Bathers*, the stern of a racing shell powered by a single rower (or, if there are more crew members, they're not in view), appears at the painting's upper-right edge; in *La Grande Jatte*, Seurat presents another shell, this time in its entirety, with a four-strong crew and (female) cox. That butterfly, along with other details, offers a grace note akin to the tabs of the central figure's boots in the *Bathers*. In the foreground of *La Grande Jatte*, Seurat again positions a reclining man. Further off, he adapts the hollering bather on the right of the earlier painting, transforming him into a clothed, elongated and helmeted youth. Seen in profile facing to the right, he holds to his lips not his hands but a brass instrument, the sound of which seems to have prompted two nearby soldiers to stand to attention.

The comparison between these hatted youths is revealing. The boy in the *Bathers* has a lyrical aura: 'He is the most poetic image ... in the *Baignade*,' declared the British art historian (and former director of the National Gallery) Kenneth Clark, 'and I have a feeling that some day I shall find his prototype in antique painting.'[26] The horn-blower in *La Grande Jatte*, though, is jerkier and more jokey, and implies that social satire and irony are now part of Seurat's intention. Who are these promenading popinjays? They feel less substantial than the earlier bathers, more unreal and puppet-like, with the artificial presence of wheeled theatrical flats; the animation of the scene has a whirring, mechanical quality, as if Seurat had grouped together a load of wind-up toys. This air of unreality is intensified by peculiarities of scale: if, for instance, the top-hatted dandy to the left of the foreground, deliberately contrasted with the burly *canotier* (canoeist or boatman) beside him, were to stand up, he'd only reach the waist of the gentleman wearing a monocle on the painting's other side.

30 Detail of *Bathers at Asnières*: boats near La Grande Jatte

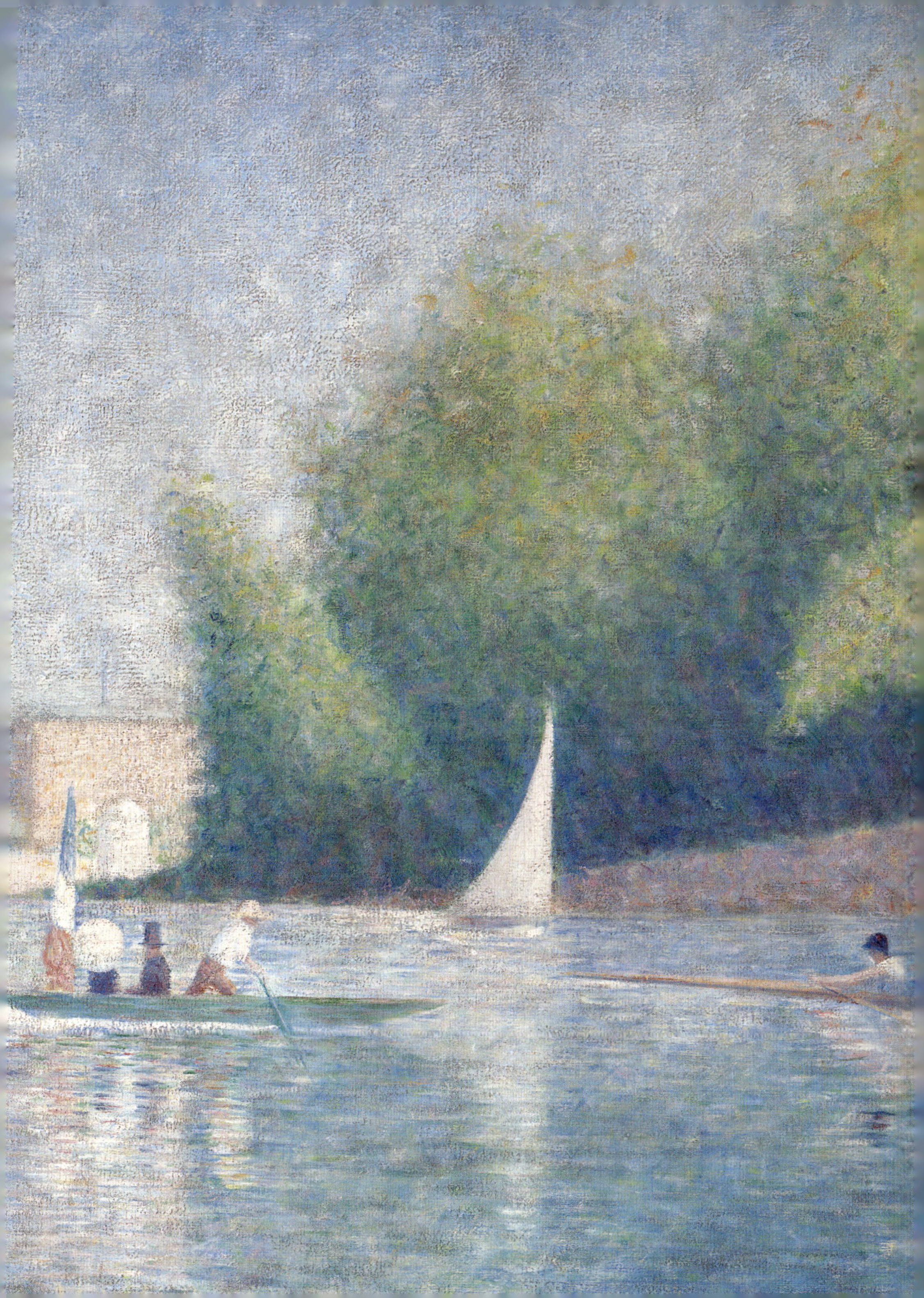

It has been suggested that, in *La Grande Jatte*, Seurat wished to lampoon bourgeois attitudes towards prostitution.[27] Is that woman with the pet monkey (a time-honoured symbol of vice) in fact a *cocotte* (an elegant 'kept woman')? What about the woman fishing to the left of the picture – is she hoping to 'catch' a client? (In French, *pêcher* means 'to fish', but *pécher* is 'to sin'.) Not every Seurat scholar buys this reading, nor is there consensus that *La Grande Jatte* is a self-consciously middle-class counterpart, even pendant, to the working-class *Bathers*. What is clear is that there is a relationship of sorts between the two works.

Which world would you prefer to visit? The genteel hubbub of *La Grande Jatte* is engrossing and entertaining; there's lots to see and decode. The lethargy of the *Bathers* might, after a while, prove draining. But it is, perhaps, a simpler place, more robust and down-to-earth, and less wickedly metropolitan: a spiritual, rather than a temporal, realm, where Seurat – as Piero had done, centuries earlier – seemingly gets to the essence of things. *Bathers at Asnières* announces Seurat's interest in fashioning a new, monumental classicism, purged of Impressionism's obsession with the momentary. But one may also wonder if it is hinting at something else. Nothing in the *Bathers* explicitly evokes the underworld. Yet the shadowy tip of La Grande Jatte, with its mysterious trees, may call to mind the *Island of the Dead* (fig. 31): Arnold Böcklin's famous motif, depicting a baleful rocky islet. The Swiss Symbolist artist painted the composition five times between 1880 and 1886, when Seurat was at work on the *Bathers*. Seurat, from 1885, was associated with various writers, including Fénéon and Kahn, linked with Symbolism, a European cultural movement that opposed empiricism and championed subjectivity to express spiritual truth.

Here, perhaps, we may be veering perilously close to fancy, but that reclining figure in the foreground of the *Bathers* – the one that's routinely compared to ancient sculptures of river gods – isn't a million miles away from an

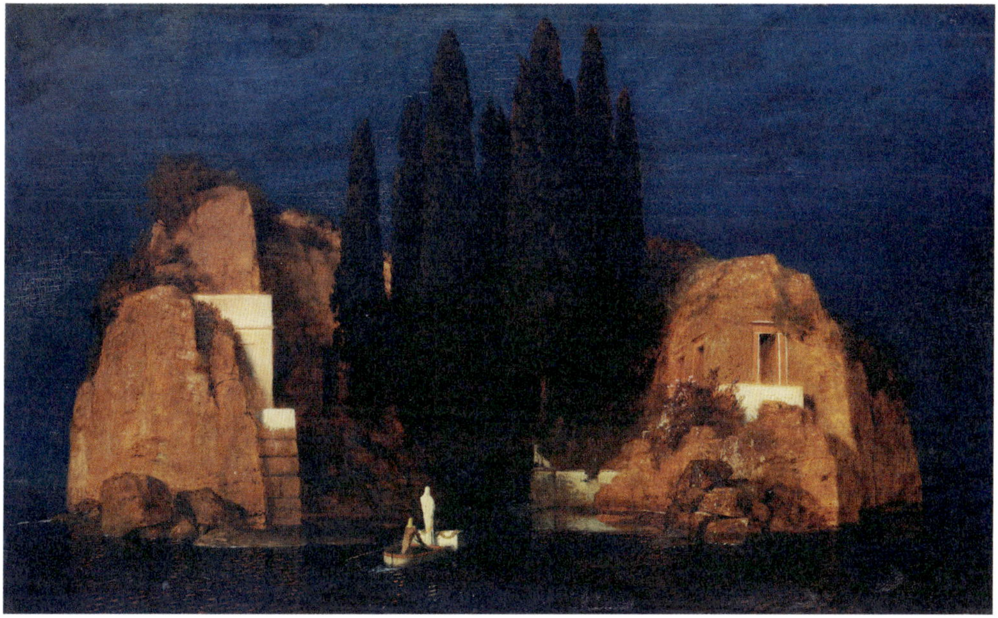

31 Arnold Böcklin (1827–1901)
Island of the Dead, 1880
Oil on wood, 73.7 × 121.9 cm
The Metropolitan Museum of Art, New York. Reisinger Fund, 1926

effigy on a tomb. Isn't his flowing, featureless white garment a little like a shroud? And doesn't the discarded item of bright clothing, in the centre of the picture, have the quality of a winding sheet, too? Could it be that the *Bathers* presents a group of men confronting the finality of life (hence its atmosphere of seriousness) – contemplating the otherworldly voyage that, one day, all alone, each of us will be forced to take? The ancients – with whom, as we have seen, Seurat was in dialogue – believed that to get to the underworld the souls of the dead had to cross the river Styx. Could this be the revelation, the epiphany, of the painting? Are Seurat's bathers waiting to see what comes next, after this life? That somnolent central figure, his shadowed face surrounded by a halo, sits upright like a newly resurrected soul. Or, if you prefer, he's simply a weary worker, not preparing to cross the Styx at all, but anticipating a dip, on a hot summer's day, in the calm, cooling waters of the Seine.

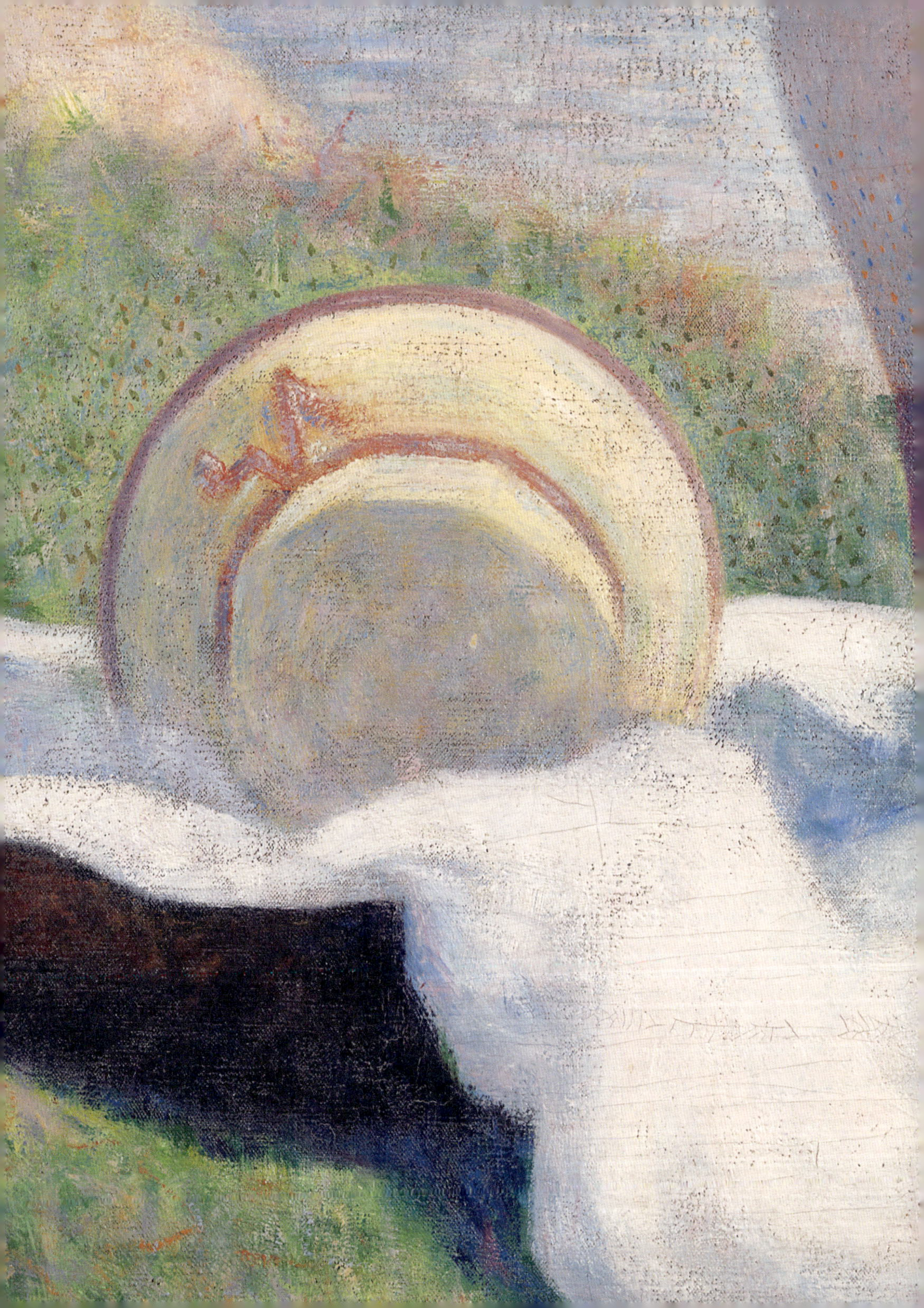

NOTES

1 Marx 1883.
2 Cooper 1945, p. 3.
3 As quoted in London 1997, p. 125.
4 After Seurat's death, the *Bathers* remained in the artist's family, before it was acquired first by the French art critic Félix Fénéon and then, in 1924, by the trustees of the Courtauld Fund, who presented it to the Tate Gallery; it was transferred to the National Gallery in 1961.
5 The other five major canvases are: *A Sunday on La Grande Jatte - 1884* (1884–6, Art Institute of Chicago); *Models* (1886–8, Barnes Foundation, Merion, Pennsylvania); *Circus Sideshow* (1887–8, The Metropolitan Museum of Art, New York); *Chahut* (1889–90, Kröller-Müller Museum, Otterlo); and *The Circus* (1891, Musée d'Orsay, Paris).
6 As quoted in Paris and New York 1991–2, p. 3.
7 Fry 1926, passim.
8 Paris and New York 1991–2, p. 6.
9 As quoted in London 1997, p. 8.
10 E.g. London 1997.
11 This letter is reproduced in full as Appendix F in Paris and New York 1991–2.
12 Jules Christophe, 'Georges Seurat', *Les Hommes d'aujourd'hui*, no. 368, 1890, n.p.; as quoted in London 1997, p. 14.
13 See the catalogue entry for *Paysage avec "Le pauvre pêcheur"* (1881) in Paris and New York 1991–2, p. 109.
14 Barron 1886, p. 40.
15 Paris and New York 1991–2, p. 150.
16 As quoted in Paris and New York 1991–2, p. 6 (and again, on p.408 of the same volume, in Anne Distel's 'Chronology').
17 E.g. London 1997, pp. 51 75.
18 The male nude, a prominent theme of ancient Greek and Roman art, was revitalised as a subject during the sixteenth century by, for instance, Michelangelo. He depicted a group of soldiers bathing naked in the river Arno in a preparatory drawing for a mural that he was commissioned to paint (but never completed) inside the council hall of Florence's Palazzo della Signoria (now Palazzo Vecchio).
19 As quoted in Paris and New York 1991–2, p. 174.
20 As quoted by, for instance, www.nationalgallery.org.uk/artists/paul-cezanne Accessed 1 November 2024
21 Paris and New York 1991–2, p. 151, n. 2 (which quotes from an article by an anonymous reviewer, published under the headline 'The Impressionist Exhibition' in New York journal *The Art Amateur,* 14 May 1886, p. 6).
22 While commenting on a draft of this text, National Gallery curator Chiara Di Stefano kindly pointed out that the Ecole des Beaux-Arts possessed nineteenth-century copies after *The Legend of the True Cross,* Piero's famous fresco cycle inside the Basilica of San Francesco in the Tuscan city of Arezzo. For further information, see Gedo 1989.
23 Ayrton 1960, p. 661.
24 Paris and New York 1991–2, p. 151.
25 E.g. London 1997, p. 75.
26 Clark 1957.
27 E.g. Smith 1997, pp. 52–60.

FURTHER READING

Ayrton 1960
M. Ayrton, 'Painting of the Month: Seurat's "Une Baignade, Asnières"', *The Listener*, 14 April 1960, pp. 660–2

Barron 1886
L. Barron, *Les Environs de Paris*, Paris 1886

Boime 1965
A. Boime, 'Seurat and Piero della Francesca', *The Art Bulletin*, 47, no. 2 (1965), pp. 265–71

Chicago 2004
R.L. Herbert (ed.), *Seurat and the Making of La Grande Jatte*, exh. cat., Art Institute of Chicago 2004, published Chicago and Berkeley

Clark 1957
K. Clark, 'Six Great Pictures, 5 – Une Baignade', *The Sunday Times*, 16 June 1957, p. 9

Clark 1984
T.J. Clark, *The Painting of Modern Life: Paris in the Art of Manet and His Followers*, New York 1984

Cooper 1945
National Gallery Archive (NGA), dossier for NG 3908: D. Cooper, 'Georges Seurat's "Une Baignade, Asnières"', in *Georges Seurat, Une baignade, Asnières, in the Tate Gallery – London, The Gallery Books No. 9*, London 1945, pp. 3–14

Fry 1926
R. Fry, *Transformations: Critical and Speculative Essays on Art*, London 1926, pp. 188–96

Gedo 1989
M.M. Gedo, 'The *Grande Jatte* as the Icon of a New Religion: A Psycho-Iconographic Interpretation', *Art Institute of Chicago Museum Studies*, 14, no. 2 (1989), pp. 222–37

Gould 1976
C. Gould, *Painting in Focus, No. 6: Seurat's 'Bathers, Asnières' and the Crisis of Impressionism*, London 1976

Grenier 1991
C. Grenier, *Seurat: Catalogue complet des peintures*, Paris 1991

London 1997
J. Leighton et al., *Seurat and The Bathers*, exh. cat., National Gallery, London 1997

Marx 1883
R. Marx, 'Le salon, VI (fin)', *Le progress artistique*, 15 June 1883

New York 2007–8
J. Hauptman (ed.), *Georges Seurat: The Drawings*, exh. cat., Museum of Modern Art, New York 2007–8

Paris and New York 1991–2
R.L. Herbert et al., *Georges Seurat, 1859–1891*, exh. cat., Galeries nationales du Grand Palais, Paris 1991; The Metropolitan Museum of Art, New York 1991–2

Smith 1997
P. Smith, *Seurat and the Avant-Garde*, New Haven and London 1997

PICTURE CREDITS

All images © The National Gallery, London, unless listed otherwise below.

Tate Gallery, on loan to the National Gallery © Tate: figs 3 and 4.

© The Metropolitan Museum of Art, New York: figs 5, 9 and 31.

© Granger/Bridgeman Images: fig. 6.

Musée d'Orsay, Paris, held at the Musée du Louvre © Grand Palais Rmn (musée d'Orsay)/Michel Urtado: fig. 7; © Grand Palais Rmn (musée d'Orsay) /Michèle Bellot: fig. 24.

Musée du Louvre, Paris © Grand Palais Rmn (musée du Louvre)/Gérard Blot: fig. 10.

The Courtauld Gallery, London (Samuel Courtauld Trust) Photo © The Courtauld/Bridgeman Images: fig. 11.

Private collection © Art Heritage/Alamy Stock Photo: fig. 12.

Troyes, musée d'Art modern © Grand Palais Rmn/Gérard Blot: fig. 14.

Musée d'Orsay, Paris © Musée d'Orsay, Dist. Grand Palais Rmn/Patrice Schmidt: figs 15 and 25.

Musée Bonnat-Helleu, Bayonne © Grand Palais Rmn/René-Gabriel Ojeda: fig. 16.

Musée Carnavalet, Histoire de Paris © Mairie de Paris, Photothèque des Musées de la ville de Paris: fig. 17.

Private Collection. On long-term loan to The Courtauld Gallery, London © The Courtauld/Bridgeman Images: fig. 19.

© The Art Institute of Chicago: figs 21 and 29.

Scottish National Gallery © National Galleries of Scotland: fig. 22.

Private Collection, New York © Photo courtesy of the owner: fig. 23.

Glasgow Museums: Art Gallery & Museums, Kelvingrove © CSG CIC Glasgow Museums Collection/Bridgeman Images: fig. 26.

Alastair Sooke is an author and broadcaster, and chief art critic at *The Telegraph*. He has written and presented more than 60 hours of television and radio for the BBC, and authored several books including a study of Henri Matisse and a history of Pop Art. He was educated at the University of Oxford and the Courtauld Institute of Art.

Authorised Representative in the EU details: Easy Access System Europe, Mustamäe tee 50, 10621 Tallinn, Estonia
gpsr.requests@easproject.com

First published in 2025 by
National Gallery Global Limited
Trafalgar Square
London WC2N 5DN
www.shop.nationalgallery.org.uk

ISBN: 978 1 85709 747 4
1057194

British Library Cataloguing-in-Publication Data
A catalogue record is available from the British Library

Publisher: Laura Lappin
Senior Project Editor: Anna Godfrey
Copy-editor: Faye Robson
Picture Researcher: Suzanne Bosman
Production: Jane Hyne

Designed by Sandra Zellmer
Origination by DL Imaging, London
Printed in Italy by Printer Trento

All works are by Georges Seurat (1859–1891) unless otherwise stated.

All measurements give height before width.

Cover and pp. 4, 16, 57, 60: details from Georges Seurat, *Bathers at Asnières*, 1884 (fig. 1)

MIX
Paper | Supporting responsible forestry
FSC® C015829
FSC
www.fsc.org